CW01457599

PORT VALE GRASS ROOTS

From Supporter To Groundsman And Back Again

Denis Dawson

CHELL PUBLICATIONS

PORT VALE
GRASS ROOTS

First published in November 1997 by Chell Publications, 17 Sprinkbank Road, Chell, Stoke-on-Trent, ST6 6HH, England. Tel.(01782) 819281.

Copyright © 1997, Denis Dawson.

ISBN 0 9532090 0 8

Cover concept: Jeff Kent.
Cover artwork: Ken Longmore.
Editor: Jeff Kent.
Editorial adviser: Rosalind Kent.
Typeset, printed and bound by: PKA Print & Design, 5-7 Dunning Street, Tunstall, Stoke-on-Trent, ST6 5AP. Tel. (01782) 575280 & 837960.

ACKNOWLEDGEMENTS
I should like to give special thanks to the following people:
Jeff Kent, for guidance and editing my book. It is fair to say that without Jeff's help the book would not have been published;
My wife Mable and my daughter Jackie, who at first thought I was kidding when I said I was going to write this book, but who committed many hours to typing my work;
Craig, my son-in-law, and his school friend Simon, who set up my computer and helped me with many related problems.
I should also like to express my thanks to the following for their invaluable assistance in the production of this book:
Neil Aspin, Mick Cullerton, Ken Longmore, Wade Martin, John Rudge, Phil Sherwin and Allan Staples.

PHOTOGRAPH CREDITS
The following people kindly supplied photographs for use in this book:
Bill Bache – front cover, back cover, 28; Denis Dawson – 1, 2, 13; Colin Askey – 3, 6, 11; Ken Griffiths – 4; May Turner – 5, 7, 8; Harry Poole – 9; Terry Miles – 10; Ken Hancock – 12; Phil Sproson – 14; Bill Lodey/Port Vale F.C. – 15-20, 22-25; Steve Speed – 21; Jayne Pattison – 26; Neil Hughes/Port Vale F.C. – 27.

All rights reserved. No part of this publication may be reproduced, stored in a retrieval system or transmitted in any form or by any means, electronic, mechanical, photocopying, recording or otherwise without the prior permission in writing of the publisher.

This book is sold subject to the condition that it shall not, by way of trade or otherwise, be lent, resold, hired out or otherwise circulated without the publisher's prior written consent in any form of binding or cover other than that in which it is published and without a similar condition including this condition being imposed on the subsequent purchaser.

Dedicated to my late father, the Vale mascot, and to my late brother, Eric, who was throughout his life the greatest Vale fan in my family.

Contents

1

My Old Dad

My old man said, 'Follow the van and . . . '
No! No! No!
My old dad said, 'Follow the Vale
and don't dilly-dally on the way.'
So off I went with my money in my pocket.
I saw the match, but I pretty soon forgot it.
They dillied, dallied, shillied and shallied,
lost their way to goal many times.
But I've been back many times for more.
God bless my old dad!

2

My Dad The Cheerleader

My dad's support for Port Vale began when he was a teenager. He went to the matches in those days with the only other member of his family who was interested in the Vale. This was his brother Fred and he too, like my dad, remained a lifelong supporter. Dad did not say a lot about his early days supporting the club, but one thing he did tell me was that he never went near the ground for one and a half seasons, and I think that this was the 1936-1937 season and part way into the 1937-1938 season. This was because the club had been relegated to the Third Division and he disagreed with the way in which the club was being run. The leading scorer, Tom Nolan, had been sold and several other established players had departed. However, as a long period in my life up to 1939 was spent in hospital, I do not know how keen Dad's support was and with the outbreak of the war I heard very little about the Vale. Then one day in 1945, he quietly announced that he was going to take my brothers and me to see the Vale for the first time.

At that time we lived in the village of Werrington at number 7, Hillside Bungalow, Washerwall Lane. Right opposite our bungalow was a piece of spare ground where my dad used to gather up all the boys of the village to play either cricket or football and, during those games, he was not only our father but a father to most of the boys. He made the bats and the wickets for cricket and supplied the balls. Looking back, I think the old bugger made up some of the rules as well! One rule I well remember was the one where if there was doubt about leg before wicket, he would say turn your bat upside down and face three balls, using just the bat handle to defend your wicket.

My earliest recollections of football were playing with a ball made out of sack bags and stuffed with either straw or hay. After the war was over, you could not buy footballs because in those days the outer case was made of leather and a rubber bladder was used on the inside to inflate the ball, and both the leather and the rubber were in very short supply. So what my dad did was to cut two large round pieces, about ten inches in diameter, of the strong sack bagging and sew them on the outside and stuff either straw or hay into them. We had hour after hour of good fun playing football this way. However, one day my dad was with a group of lads, when he said, 'I'll go up to the Vale next week and see if they will sell us a proper ball.' This he did and they told him to go back the following week and they would see what they could do. So he went back up to the Old Recreation Ground in Hanley and returned with two outer cases, but no bladders, because they said they simply could not obtain enough of these even for themselves. Those two outer cases were a real work of art. What the club had done was to take them to a cobbler and have them restitched where required, and on the very weak places they had large black patches stitched on. Then my dad had a brain wave and decided not to stuff them with hay or straw, but to put two large cycle inner tubes into them and see how they looked. This he did and, although they were far from round, they were a big improvement on our sack bag ball. Our first job before playing with our new ball was to go through the village to show it to all who were interested. At every stop we said, 'Billy Pointon's kicked this ball, Alf Bellis kicked this ball and Bob Pursell,' and so it went on and on.

Now many people have told me over the years that my dad was a real character. He had a very rough and deprived childhood, as did many of that time, and whenever he saw any child in distress or deprived, he would take him to one side, talk to him and try to help him out. Also, he got all the lads of the village together to play and talk and he was a cheerleader at the Vale. This is what I hope they have meant by a character. Despite saying that, I could understand my mother's feelings towards my dad becoming Port Vale's cheerleader. I will mention just one or two nasty remarks which were directed at my dad when people saw him doing his rounds of the ground all dressed up in his undertaker's top hat and frock-tail coat and carrying his brolly. 'Fancy dressing up like that and making an exhibition of himself. He must be bloody crackers,' was a very common view. 'He should be locked up and the key thrown away,' was another thing I heard. 'I would not subject my family to ridicule by going about like that,' was yet another thing, and when we were at Leicester City for a match and he was going round the pitch, someone in the ground started to throw fireworks at him. He managed to fend some off with his brolly and tried to jump out of the way of those which landed near to his feet. Eventually the police moved in to advise him to leave because things were getting out of hand. As he did so a lad in the crowd shouted out, 'Leave the bloody idiot where he is. It's better than paying to watch a clown in a circus!' Readers may think that's funny, but the words 'idiot' and 'clown' stuck in my craw.

3

One of the funny things which was said occurred at a home match. I was standing on the Lorne Street side of the ground when my dad commenced his walk around the pitch. As he approached the area near to where we were standing, a chap in front of me turned round to face the opposite direction and said to those standing near to him, 'Tell me when he has gone well past.' When my dad had disappeared, he turned back round and said, 'That man looks really ill. He scares me to death. It will not be long before a real undertaker is looking after him!' Well, the laugh here is that my dad was still alive and kicking some twenty years later and was riding a bike three months before he died at the age of almost eighty. A comment that never failed to crop up whenever we visited London for matches, but which was never said with malice, was, 'Cor blimey, the undertaker is here again! Have you come to bury them mate?'

Dad became the cheerleader as a result of a bit of fun between him and a chap by the name of Joe Lymer, who was a local undertaker and also a Vale supporter. When Dad first mentioned it to us he said, 'Joe is a bugger for a bit of fun, but he is not catching me on this one.' A dapper little fellow by the name of George Grocott was doing the cheerleader's job at the time, but because, I think, of the insults hurled at him when he went round the track, George would sometimes swear back. Some people said that they knew George reckoned that he liked a drink before the match and this made him worse. Well, I was given to understand that my dad and Joe discussed my dad becoming the new cheerleader as they were travelling back from an away match.

One night after he had had his tea Dad said to my mother, 'I am going down to Joe Lymer's, but I won't be long.'

'Joe Lymer's?' she said. 'What on earth are you going there for?'

'You'll see when I get back,' he replied and off he went. About two hours later he returned carrying a very large suitcase, a big brown bag and something long wrapped up in brown paper. He lifted the suitcase on to the table and opened it with great pride. Out of it came a pair of pin-striped trousers, a black waistcoat and two frock-tail coats. Next onto the table went the big brown bag and out of that he took a top hat. Then came the long parcel. He unwrapped this and out came a huge umbrella.

'What is that lot?' my mother asked.

'You'll see in a few weeks' time,' he replied. 'I told you I was going to be Port Vale's cheerleader didn't I? Well that lot is my gear.'

My mother's face was something I will never forget. She was completely gobsmacked and did not reply.

4

My dad's next job was to go out and get stacks of the best quality black and white wool that money could buy and for about a month he worked on the gear every spare minute that he could muster. He put 'P.V.F.C.' and Staffordshire knots on the top hat and 'Nil desperandum' on the front of it.

'Nil desperandum. What does that mean Dad?' I enquired.

'You thick sod! Haven't you learned anything at school?' With a touch of pride and arrogance he dragged the words out: 'Nil desperandum means never despair and if you support the Vale as long as I have you'll learn the true meaning of that!'

As the seasons have gone by I really have learned the truth of that only too well. He completed the work on his gear and I have to say he made a smashing job of the lot.

Dad put the gear on and I thought he looked just great. Because of this and as he was going to be a much bigger part of the Vale than he had been on the terraces I saw nothing wrong in what he was doing.

When my mother saw him kitted out she was absolutely astonished and her face was a picture that no artist could paint.

'You're not going to ride up and down on the buses dressed up in that lot are you?' she eventually managed to ask.

'Well you don't think that I am going to walk to the matches do you?' he replied.

'Well,' she said. 'Having got over the initial shock, you look like the organ grinder's monkey. How on earth shall I be able to face the neighbours? You will not get me side by side with you with that lot on!'

Until then after most matches my mother had met him in Hanley to have a short walk around the town and to go to the Theatre Royal or the pictures if there was anything good on, but that was the end of that.

My dad's response to her outburst was to tell her: 'Look, what I'm doing is nothing more than a little harmless fun. I do not come out of the public house at closing time on Saturday nights making a nuisance of myself and cursing and fighting like a lot that I know.'

Well I have thought a lot about this as the years have rolled by and I cannot say that he was wrong in what he said, but I have to say that I can well understand my mother's feelings. She was a very quiet and reserved person who did not go about the place shouting her mouth off and she did not want to see her family sneered at. However, she eventually came to terms with the situation and she probably realised in the end that all the members of her family were Vale daft.

3

The Beginning Of My Love Affair

When you start to support a football team it's a bit like getting married. You marry, or you should marry, the one you love and I reckon that you love your football team in the same way, for better or for worse. Better when your team is doing well; worse when you are in the doldrums. And to death us do part, without a doubt!

My love affair with Port Vale started way back in 1944, just after my 12th birthday.

'I'll take you three lads to see Port Vale,' said my old dad out of the blue.

"Port Vale". Those two words struck a chord in my heart and have done ever since. So Saturday came and my dad, my elder brother Eric, my younger brother Les and I were on our way.

'Who are we playing?' asked Eric.

'West Bromwich Albion,' replied my dad. 'But it's only more or less a friendly. League football doesn't start until next year.'

Wartime football I think they called it then.

West Bromwich Albion was another name which struck the same kind of chord that Port Vale had. The funny thing is I don't remember a lot about the game itself and yet I can recall some of the Vale players who appeared that day, such as Harry Prince (the goalkeeper) and Alf Bellis (the outside-left). However, remember the game or not, that day started me on my way to being a lifelong Vale supporter. In those days my dad couldn't afford to take us to see many games and so my real support started on Saturday 28th September 1946 when Vale played at home against Swindon Town. The Vale team for that match was:

1
Heppell

2   3
Pursell   Chew

4   5   6
Hallam   Griffiths   McGarry

7   8   9   10   11
Byrne   Lyman   Davies   Jones W.M.   Bellis

The programme of this match is still in my possession, although by the time the game was played, Les had lost interest and did not regain it until a few years later. Then he became as big a supporter as the rest of us. To be able to attend matches, I had to raise my own money. Near to us was a farm where they kept pigs and they took all the scraps that they could get to help to feed them. For these scraps, they gave us 2s. 6d. per fortnight. Admission to the ground was 6d. for juniors (the equivalent of 2½p now), a programme was 2d. and after the match we bought 3 pennies' worth of chips from Derricots Chip Shop, which was near to the Hanley ground, and so the scraps were more than enough to pay my way.

The first cup match that I saw the Vale play was the Sentinel Cup Final in 1946. It was Port Vale "A" versus Stoke City "B" and the Vale won 5-0! In goal for the Vale that night was a chap named Alex Humphreys who later became a Stoke City director and who I later learnt had created a Sentinel Cup record by winning a medal for both Stoke City and Port Vale in this competition. The first F.A. Cup match I saw was on a Monday afternoon in January 1946. That was Vale versus Bradford Park Avenue. The Vale had lost 2-1 at Bradford on the Saturday and this was the second leg. My father took me along, but laid down the law to Eric that he was not to skip work in order to see the match. We had been on the ground about ten minutes and I casually turned around to see my brother just a few steps behind us. He made a very quick exit, but at night when my dad was talking about the match he kept butting in only to break off very quickly. My dad thought our goalie, Arthur Jepson, had made a hash of one of the goals and he thought the Bradford keeper, Chick Farr, had played a great game, which was completely the opposite of what my brother thought. After Eric had butted in once too often, my dad asked rather harshly, 'Have I been to this match or have you been? Or are you psychic?' End of discussion!

One of the most outstanding memories I have of watching the Vale play in Hanley is of a player by the name of Cliff Pinchbeck. He was a six foot centre-forward who was about 15 stones and as strong as an ox. We played Brighton and Hove Albion at home in October 1949 and Cliff was in the opposing team. He was the star turn, even though Vale won 3-0. A Brighton player went down injured and after treating him, the Brighton trainer came round the back of the goal net which was very close to where the spectators were. As he did so, a wag in the crowd shouted, 'Give you £500 for your centre-forward, mate.'

Back came the reply, 'You can have that bugger for nowt as far as I'm concerned.'

12 days later, Vale signed him for £3,500. We were at home the following Saturday against Millwall and Malcolm Finlayson, who later played for Wolves, was the visiting keeper. What a game our Cliff played! Wham! A hat trick for Cliff in his first game for us, but two years later he didn't report for pre-season training and claimed to be ill. Although he regained his place when he finally turned up, that autumn he was sold to Northampton Town.

Another story I have to tell from my early days as a supporter concerned our goalkeeper, George Heppell. We were playing Hyde United in a Cheshire League fixture and George came striding into his goal as he always did, bent down with his back to us and placed his cap and gloves behind the goal post. As he did so, one of the mob that we were with said, 'Well, bloody hell, the dirty sod. Just look at that!'

'Look at what?' one of us asked, to which he replied, 'My mate said that boys who masturbate grow into men with lumps behind their ears and just look at that lump behind his ear, the dirty sod!' I like to think that I didn't believe this story, but I have always looked for lumps behind the ears and I've always wondered when I've seen them!

I have many fond memories of the days in Hanley, the last being the final game versus Aldershot, which we lost 1-0. When I go to Hanley shopping centre, I always try to park my car so that I can walk along the path that is adjacent to Weatherby's potbank and goes past where the Swan Passage side of the ground was. The path overlooks the new shopping complex which is built on a part of the old ground and a short distance away is St. John's Church. If I'm with a member of my family, I will always stop and recall the day when I saw Ronnie Allen put a penalty kick out of the ground and straight into the churchyard. This was in a cup tie against Finchley, a team of amateurs, which we won 5-0.

4

Mixed Memories!

The first game at Vale Park was versus Newport County on 24th August 1950 and we won 1-0, with Walter Aveyard being the scorer. Before the match there was community singing, with Fodens Motor Works Band being conducted by Arthur Cager, who stood on a rostrum just as he did before every F.A. Cup Final at Wembley. Unfortunately, there were many problems with the drainage and the subsoil of the pitch at Vale Park, which led to matches being postponed and on Christmas Day 1950, Stoke City came to our aid by loaning us their ground for a match against Bristol Rovers. Before the Blackpool cup tie in 1954, you just could not pull a roller through the middle of the pitch and what the groundsman, Len Parton, did was enlist the help of volunteers to pull a 9 foot plank with a hole in each end and a rope through the holes. The plank was pulled across the ground in order to get it flat and it was amazing how well this worked. Another great effort was needed to get the ground ready for a match versus Fulham. The chairman hired staff from the Parks Department to put 200 tons of sand onto the pitch. Neither the Fulham manager nor the captain that day, the England international, Johnny Haynes, were very keen to play, but play they did.

Yet another game which took a lot of preparation was a cup tie against Aston Villa in February 1960. On this occasion, staff hired from the Parks Department, reinforced by volunteers, worked under the floodlights throughout the night to get the pitch fit. One particular area of concern was just in front of the press box on the Lorne Street side of the ground. Many tons of sand were put onto this area to try and dry it out and the following day when the match was played, every time the flying Villa winger Peter McParland got the ball, he just could not get through that patch. Consequently, it became nicknamed by many who worked on the ground that night "The Peter McParland patch"! For that match everyone who had helped to get the ground ready was given free tickets.

Some of the matches which stand out most in my memory are for some reason mainly away matches. One afternoon in 1953, my dad, my brother Eric and I went to see the Vale play at Chesterfield. We took our places in the stand and my dad soon became engaged in football chatter

9

with a Chesterfield supporter who sat next to him, and this chap was enthusing about their left-winger, Alf Bellis.

'Can't tell me much about him,' my dad said. 'He played for us until we sold him to Bury.'

'Must have been crazy,' said the Chesterfield fan. 'If he was a younger man, he could in my opinion be an England international.'

'Never in a million years,' replied my dad.

'Well, you'll see this afternoon,' said the Chesterfield chap.

Every time Alf got the ball during the game, he shouted, 'Go on Alf! Go on Alf! Go on Alf!' He got really excited, he did. With about five minutes of the match remaining and the Vale leading 2-1, Alf got the ball and was off up the wing like an express train. Our friend leaped up on his feet, with his hat in his hands, and shouted his head off. 'Go on Alf! Go on Alf! Go on Alf! Skin 'em! Show 'em your arse!' Real gone he was, but as Alf tried to enter the penalty area, over came our full-back Stan Turner and crash, the ball landed in the crowd. Completely exhausted, the chap sat down and replaced his hat, but as Alf came within earshot of the stand, once again our little friend got up. 'Hey Bellis,' he yelled. 'Next match stay at home and dig the garden. You would be better with a bloody muck fork in your hand than a football at your feet! Bloody well let us down today you have, but then you've never been much good!'

'Well, I don't believe you,' said my dad. 'An international one minute, a nobody the next. You fickle sod!'

In 1954, Cardiff City were in the First Division and boasted a string of Welsh internationals, two of whom I can still recall, Alf Sherwood and the great Trevor Ford. There had been a bit of hassle between the two clubs prior to the fourth round cup match being played. If there was to be a replay, the Vale wanted it to be played on a Monday, with the kickoff at 2 p.m. 'No!' said Cardiff City. After Cardiff had won their appeal to the F.A., it was to be played on the Thursday. The trip down to Wales by train was a nightmare because we didn't know whether the match would be played due to heavy snow and frost. However, we were relieved when we got there and the match had been declared on, although the pitch was rock hard because of the frost.

The Vale lads played their hearts out that day in Cardiff. Internationals or not, the home side hardly ever got near our goal. Now the Vale supporters, and my dad in particular, were very peeved at the F.A.'s decision to play the match on the Thursday and at every opportunity Dad kept having a dig at Cardiff supporters, doing so in as good an imitation

Welsh voice as he could. Because they were playing so poorly, it began to get to them. The Vale went 2 goals up and, try as hard as he could, their hero, Trevor Ford, couldn't get near enough to our goal to cause us any problems. During the last 15 minutes or so of the game, every time their wingers got the ball, up went the cry, 'Give it to Trevor! Give it to Trevor!' Yes, they really thought, even at that late stage, that Trevor was going to save their bacon. During one spell of Cardiff pressure, Trevor made a complete hash of a cross from one of the wingers and up stood my dad who shouted, 'Give it to Trevor! Him a Welsh international? You make me laugh. He couldn't kick my arse!'

This really got to them, with the game into its final seconds. Then my dad got up again and shouted, 'Replay on Thursday, boys. 2 p.m. kickoff. Don't be late and don't forget to bring Trevor with you!' This was more than our Welsh friends could take. There was snow lying on the terraces and snowballs were flying at us from all angles. When the final whistle sounded we made our way to the exit and, as we did so, a squeaky little Welsh voice came over the Tannoy system: 'Please, please, please go along home quietly, boys, and don't attack the visiting supporters.'

If there had not been a strong police presence outside the ground, we would have got murdered, for there was violence in those days just as there is now, but it gets more media coverage now than it did then. However, as it turned out, we got to the railway station safely with a police escort.

The season 1953-1954 saw the Vale enjoy a great F.A. Cup run, culminating in their appearance at Villa Park facing West Brom in a semi-final. Well, the critics wrote us off, just as they had done when we had faced Blackpool in the fifth round at Vale Park, but they had once again underrated the battling quality of the Vale lads of that time. It's fair to say that we completely outplayed West Brom in every department, so much so that I was later told that the West Brom chairman had left his seat in the directors' box some twenty minutes before the final whistle, having accepted in his mind that we were going to win the match. The way in which we lost that match was nothing short of a disgrace and daylight robbery. Playing for West Brom that day was an ex-Vale player, Ronnie Allen, who, because he had been born in Newhouse Road, Bucknall, was a local hero, but it was this very man who brought about our downfall, which occurred by very unfair means. To put it bluntly, we were cheated. Albion's George Lee was well outside the Vale penalty area when he was tackled by our centre-half, Tommy Cheadle, and what he did

11

was to take a great dive which took him not into our box, but just onto the line. The ref, who had given some very strange decisions, could not point to the spot quickly enough and seconds later Ronnie Allen put the ball in the back of the net. To say that the player took a dive is spot on and as I was at the end where the penalty was given and looking right across the eighteen-yard line, I know that decision was nothing short of cheating and worse was to follow near the end when we scored a great goal only for the linesman to flag offside when in fact the scorer, Albert Leake, was well onside. Some people who read this and who saw the Middlesbrough versus Chesterfield cup semi-final in April 1997 will have seen for themselves just what the man in the middle can do one way or another and there is nothing that the injured party can do about it.

We went to Liverpool on Easter Monday 1955 to play a league fixture. On the previous Friday, we had played them at home and an ex-Liverpool player, Cyril Done, had scored four goals for us in a 4-3 victory. So I suppose the Liverpool fans were feeling a little bit peeved. Anyway, during the pre-match kick-in, up kept going the chant 'Liverpool reject' every time that Cyril touched the ball. During the game, Liverpool were leading 1-0 when the Vale were awarded a spot kick. Up stepped our Cyril and bang into the back of the net the ball landed. My dad shouted, 'Hey! What about that, you Scousers? Not bad for a Liverpool reject!'

Cups came at us from all directions, and I mean real cups because in those days they served whatever beverage you had in earthenware cups. Amazingly, however, no injuries occurred and near to the end of the match a police officer came over to us and asked my dad, 'Are you lot together?'

'Yes,' he replied.

'Have you come by car, coach or train?'

My dad said, 'Yes, the train. It departs at 6.15 p.m.'

'Then,' said the police officer, 'it's only a short way to the station, so you'll have plenty of time to get there. So hang on here a while until the ground has cleared and all is quiet outside. Then make your way out of the ground and go quietly to the station. I want no trouble here.'

'Well, you won't get any from us,' replied my dad.

We waited a little while until all had gone quiet outside, or so we thought, but as we made our way through the exit doors, without a policeman in sight, we saw this big mob of Liverpool supporters. One was in his shirt sleeves, shadow-boxing just as boxers do before a fight.

'Hey up!' went the cry. 'The three musketeers. Come on you bastards, let us see if you can fight like the three musketeers,' said the guy in shirt sleeves.

'Keep your cool lads, walk slowly and look straight ahead,' said my dad, trying to act bravely.

My brother Eric, who was an amateur boxer, did not seem bothered at all. In fact, he seemed to relish the thought of having a do even if the odds were against us. Me, well I was the non-fighter in our house. My idea of self-defence in those days was to lay hold of something heavy and let 'em have it, or give them a swift kick in the balls. If I could have done a Superman act at that moment I would have zoomed right over that big bad mob, leaving behind me any soft bugger who wanted to fight.

However, reality wasn't like that and I had to start thinking what part I was going to play in this little scene. Well, talk about hiding behind your mother's apron strings, I did better than that. My youngest brother, Len, was with us and in a flash I'd got it. I'd look after our young Len and let those two soft buggers fight if they wanted to. As we got near to the mob, they closed in on us.

'Get the old bastard's brolly,' shouted someone. This was done and it lay in a crumpled mess on the ground. 'Knock his fucking hat off and crush it,' someone else shouted.

The hat was knocked off, but for some miraculous reason suffered little damage and someone picked it up and handed it back to me. The fight itself was a nonevent. So close were those bodies that not one real blow could be struck and now came the strangest sight that you could imagine. About a dozen or maybe more big strong youths pushed their way through the mob. Some grabbed my dad, some grabbed Eric and others pushed me and Len along, and not one hand in the mob was raised to stop them.

'On the train?' asked one of the gang.

'Yes,' we said in chorus.

'Let us get you there safe and sound then,' they said.

As we walked to the station, my dad asked, 'What's your motive in all this lot?'

'Oh, we are Everton supporters and do not like our city getting a bad name, nor do we like to see visiting supporters set about,' they said.

I was never so relieved in all my life that I was on that train and on my way home. When talking about this to my mother the same night, my dad said pointing to me, 'I didn't see you getting involved this afternoon.'

'Hang on a bit,' I retorted. 'I looked after your hat and saved it from ruin and I looked after our young Len. He could have been trampled to death if I hadn't been there.'

'Well, I'm glad one of the family has got a bit of sense!' piped up my mother. 'Grown men going to football matches and fighting. I can't understand you!' she said. At that moment I certainly felt less of a coward than I had done earlier.

We went to see a cup tie at Barnsley in January 1957 and Harry Poole was playing up front and having a great game, much to the delight of our dad and all the other Vale fans. The Vale supporters who liked to see football played the way it should be, loved to see Harry Poole. Once again my dad was making himself heard and he was having a go at the Barnsley centre-half who was trying to kick our Harry into orbit. My dad did not like this one bit. We were well into the match when a female Barnsley supporter behind us shouted, 'Hey, you with that big fucking daft hat on, fucking shut up right now or I will stuff your fucking big hat down your fucking throat or up your fucking arse, you big daft Vale bastard!'

My dad took no notice at all, but a few minutes later she sneaked up behind him and pushed the hat off and looked as though she was going to jump all over it and flatten it. But before she could so, my brother Eric, who feared no-one, stopped her and other Barnsley yobs who were going to join in. He retrieved the hat and handed it back to my dad, who, after calmly replacing it on his head, turned to the "lady" and said, 'I have earned my living down the pits all my life, but I have never heard miners curse better than you have just now. You do yourself nor the place of your birth any credit at all, you dirty-mouthed bitch!'

I thought, oh my god, we're going to get lynched here, but to my great surprise not one voice was raised in her defence. As we made our way to the exit at the end of the match, a Barnsley supporter came up to my dad and said, 'I hope you're not going back home with the impression that we are all like her. She's here at every game,' he said, 'and she's always the same.'

'Well, of course I won't,' replied my dad.

We went to Oldham, one Saturday, to watch a league match and part way through the game my dad needed to go to the toilet. He handed his brolly and top hat to Eric to look after, and off he went. He had not been gone long when there was a commotion going on behind us and something was being tossed in the air, from one spectator to another. Had someone not shouted, 'Hey up, lads! We've got the cheerleader's "kegs"!', we should not have known what was going through the air.

14

'Bloody hell!' my brother said. 'They have got the old man's trousers!'

He gave the hat and brolly to me to hold and set off to retrieve the trousers, which he did without too much trouble. Had my dad not got his trousers back, I could not imagine a funnier sight than him boarding the coach for home with his top hat and frock-tailed coat, and his umbrella held aloft, with just his long johns for bottom cover. I think it would have made the national press!

My brother Len and my dad went by train to watch the Vale play at Bristol City in October 1960. Late in the second half, the Vale were losing 3-1, but our left-winger, Dennis Fidler, began to skin the Bristol full-back and the Vale pulled the game back. Len was so excited that he was completely shattered and fell fast asleep soon after their train left Bristol. When he woke up, the old man and this Irish chap were going at it hammer and tongs on politics. Len had not been awake many minutes when the train slowed down and pulled into a station. He looked out of the window, hoping they were at Stoke Station and what a shock awaited him. 'Bloody hell Dad!' he roared. 'We are at Crewe!' They got off the train there and had to wait two and a half hours for a train back to Stoke! Well, my dad was a bugger to argue politics with and he very rarely lost an argument, but I think it's fair to say that on this rare occasion he lost hands down. Anyway I bet the Irish chap thought so too!

5

Enter The Groundsman

I was the area foreman for the Burslem, Smallthorne and Norton areas of the City Parks Department when the Vale groundsman job became vacant. One afternoon, I was going through Burslem Park on my way to check out some of the work being done in my area. Len Parton, the Vale groundsman at that time, was sitting on a seat near the bowls pavilion, watching a game of bowls. When he saw me, he called me over.

'How would you like to become the Vale groundsman?' he enquired. 'You see,' he continued, 'it does not matter who knows, but I am leaving in two weeks' time to look after Stoke City's pitch. As you know, they have just had it re-turfed.'

'Would I like to be the Vale's groundsman?' I replied. 'You bet I would! Next best thing,' I said, 'to putting a number 7 shirt on!'

'I thought you would,' he replied. 'I've had a word with Alderman Barber, the ground director, and he would love to see you there. However,' he continued, 'it'll have to be advertised in the "Sentinel" because if you do take the job, the Alderman does not want it to be thought that he has poached you from your present job, him being a member of the City Council, you see.'

'Don't worry,' I said, 'my application will be the first on Norman Jones' desk,' and I duly posted it that night. In due course, I received a reply requesting me to attend for an interview at 1.30 p.m. on 14 June 1966.

The interview was conducted by the club chairman, Fred Pinfold, Alderman Barber and the club secretary, Norman Jones. This took about twenty minutes and at the end of the interview, I was told the job was mine if I wanted it, no danger there. I went onto the pitch with the Alderman and he informed me there and then that he liked to be known as such. By this time, Len Parton had been gone about three weeks, the grass had not been cut for three weeks prior to him leaving and the newly seeded area up to the middle had not been rolled.

'That area up the middle,' I said to the Alderman, 'urgently wants rolling.'

'How soon can you do that?' he asked.

Well, the day of the interview, we had moved house from Ball Green

16

to my present home at Chell. I had been up from about 6 in the morning and, upon leaving the house for the interview, I had promised my wife that I would soon be back to help her sort things out. Sort things out at home! No chance! There was only one thing on my mind at that moment, my pitch. So I told my new ground director that as soon as I had been home to tell my family, I would be back to roll the newly seeded area. I duly arrived home and told the family. 'But,' I said, 'I have got to go back to sort one or two things out, but I should not be too long.'

'Hope not,' said the wife. 'We have got such a lot of sorting out to do.'

I did the rolling on my own with a roller borrowed from the Parks Department and arrived home about one to two hours later, and walked right into a good ear bashing from the wife. It bloody well served me right!

'If you're starting off like this,' she said, 'goodness knows what it will be like when the season starts. We won't see much of you at all.' And how right she was.

Next morning, I was asked to go over to the ground for a photo call, and this I did feeling like someone who had just won the pools. My boss was Mr. P. Dyer, who was the chief superintendent for the whole of the Parks Department, and he came over to see me. He expressed his regret at my departure, but wished me all the best with my new job and even followed this up a couple of days later with a lovely letter. He also agreed to release me with just three days' notice, so I left my job with the Parks Department on Friday 17 June 1966 and commenced my duties as Vale's full-time groundsman.

I arrived at the ground at 8 that morning to find the place deserted except for one person, Ann Povey, whom the former groundsman always referred to as the "charlady". She let me introduce myself and made me a cup of tea and made me feel most welcome. I got the mower out of the shed and started to cut the grass, which because of its length required raking up and carting away. 9.15 arrived and I was beginning to wonder where my helpers were. At 9.30, Alderman Barber arrived on the pitch.

'Where's the lads?' I enquired.

Looking rather sheepish, he replied, 'Well, those three lads who were on the photograph with you are the ones who are helping Lol with the interior painting. In any case,' he went on, 'they are now on three weeks' holiday.'

'What about out there?' I asked.

'Well, I've got rid of the others,' he replied. 'Idle little devils they were and they would not have done you any good.'

'When then,' I asked, 'am I going to get help out here?'

'In about 3 or 4 weeks' time,' he replied. 'We've got lads coming in then from all over the place. You will manage. You've got black and white blood in your body, but take your time. You do not have to do all the work in one week.'

And so I cut up, raked and carted away the grass on my own. The lads arrived three weeks after I started and I was allocated four at that stage, two to clean up the terraces and two to help me get the pitch into shape and to paint the tunnel entrance, track wall and stand wall. The four lads allocated to me were Mick Lawton, a hard bugger of a Scouser, who has since become Mick Miller, the comedian; Ray Winskill, a lad who never played much football in a Vale shirt; Milija Aleksic, a smashing lad and a grand goalkeeper (whom Gordon Lee, later the manager, did not rate, but who later played for Luton and Spurs) and Raymond Kennedy, a Geordie. Out of all the many lads who were there at the time, Milija and Ray were the only two who really made the grade in football and yet they were never rated by the Vale!

Milija was a quick-tempered lad who could not stand fools lightly. He was also a very proud lad and then there was his dad who really looked after his son's welfare. Milija mostly managed to control his temper, although on one occasion he was a little peeved by something that I had done and in the tea room he said, 'You are a bastard, you are!'

I replied, 'It takes one to find one!' at which point he promptly stuck one on me, sending me to the floor!

So his pride and his dad were the things that were his undoing. He would not allow anyone to touch his kit. He took the lot home and washed and ironed it to perfection. He also took his bootlaces out after every game and bleached them to make them snow white!

The back room staff said things like, 'Never make a pro, he won't', 'He's a ponce, he is', 'He's a big fairy' and 'Mick Lawton and Billy McNulty are far better keepers than him'. And these were the best things you ever heard the back room mischief-makers say about him. 'Anyway,' said one of the back room staff one day, 'I've told Gordon Lee that if he signs him, he'll have his dad to contend with.'

Sadly, the manager listened to the gossip and they did not sign him, which was a stroke of good fortune for Luton Town and Spurs, but I'm proud of the fact that I am the one who put my hand on his shoulder when he left and said, 'See you in the top flight one day son.'

Now we come to Ray Kennedy. This lad upset the wrong bloke from day one and that was Lol Hamlett. From that day he could do nothing right when working inside, but when I had him outside he was great. They said they could not afford to sign Ray, but that was piffle. At the end of each season, the manager had each lad in his office to let him know whether or not he was to be kept on. At that time, along with other lads, Ray was helping to sieve soil on the track before it was put onto the pitch. He took his turn to see the manager, Sir Stanley Matthews, and was not in there long. When he returned, he sat on top of the pile of soil and, as the old saying goes, he did not know whether to laugh or cry. Presently, when he had calmed down, he said, 'I don't mind him telling me I'm out, but it's what he said to me when I asked if he could find me another club that really hurts. He said to me, "Son, I don't like to be vulgar, but I think I have got to be in your case. You will never make a pro so long as you have got a hole in your arse!" '

The problem was therefore not a lack of money, but a lack of professional judgement and Ray went on to star for Arsenal, Liverpool, Swansea and England.

When the 1966-1967 season started, the four lads became two and each helped me in turn. However, the inside staff didn't give much help. There were as many as ten in there at times and it was at this point that I began to wonder whether I had made the right decision in joining the Vale. However, worse was to follow when the lads started to play their games.

'You can't have these lads on Saturday and not a lot on weekdays,' I was told. Now I ask any sensible person how on earth can one man go onto that pitch in the middle of winter, push back all the divots and then roll it? But this was exactly what they expected and it was at that point that the arguments started.

'Len did it,' they said.

'No, he didn't,' I retorted. 'He used to have four or five blokes from the Parks Department after every match and I was sometimes one of them, and he used to give us a couple of quid each time. I have asked Norman Jones if I can do the same and he says, "No! If Len did that, he either paid it out of his own pocket or fiddled it out of the sweep money which he collects." '

After a lot of hassle, I was allocated one lad after each game and that was how it stayed for about two seasons. Then came the best bit of luck I could have wished for. A lad came onto the pitch one Saturday night and asked, 'Can I help you on here after the matches mate?'

'You can,' I replied. 'But you won't get paid. I can get you into the matches for free, but that is it.'

'It doesn't matter,' he replied. 'I am a Vale supporter and I can bring some of my mates along with me if you like.'

These lads stuck with me through thick and thin, never let me down and were still with me when I left the Vale. I think, or I like to think, that the little kick-abouts that I organised after our Sunday morning stints on the ground encouraged these lads to keep coming along, just as much as the fact that they were Vale supporters.

Some of the happiest memories of my boyhood are those when my dad used to play cricket and football with all the boys of the village and that is what I tried to do with these lads at the Vale. I had a nickname for all of them: David Small became "Shortly", David Cooper became "Cooperman" and Alan Bridge (who was a right cheeky little bugger) became "Junior" because he always called me "Grandad". But the one I liked best was Steve Moulton. This lad helped out a bit in a butcher's shop and so his nickname became "Pork Chop". There are many unsung heroes in football and these four lads were my heroes. Another helper was Terry Foster, who was a really grand sort of chap and put in many hours with me. Paul Brant also gave me a lot of his time, especially during his holidays and even once when the cup final was on. He worked with me from 9 till 5 on the Saturday, pushing the soil, which we had sieved, onto the pitch.

When the first December in the job came round, the pitch was in a right mess. Actually, the problems had started in about February the previous season and almost everyone who came into contact with me was asking, 'Why has the pitch deteriorated so badly?' I knew the exact reason. Vale's youth team were due to play Bradford City in a Youth Cup tie. Because the pitch had not had anything done on it after the previous match, it had become a rutted, frozen mess. The groundsman, Len Parton, always walked through Burslem Park on his way to work each morning and as he did so on the morning of the game, one of the lads quipped, 'No match tonight then, Len?'

'There will be,' he said. 'Them buggers over there think more about the youth team than about the first team and by hook or by crook I have got to make it playable, or I am finished.'

As I walked through the park gates at Hamil Road that same morning, on my way to check work being done in my area, I saw a highway steamroller (the biggest one that they had) going through the Railway Paddock gates. On my way back to the park, I decided to pop in to Vale Park and have a look (a nosy sod, I am), and there was the roller, watched by Len.

'I told you, didn't I!' he said. 'Lovely job that is. Flat as a pancake!' he concluded.

The roller went on its way back to the Highways depot and the rest of the day was spent by the groundstaff lads dressing the middle of the pitch with sand, but, alas, at about 4.30 p.m. down came one hell of a fog and the match had to be postponed. The story about the roller was denied by Len in the "Sentinel" when he had gone to Stoke City. I do not know why because not only had I seen that roller working there on the pitch, I had also been in conversation with the man himself while it was being done.

The next morning, as Len again passed through the park on his way to the ground, one of the Parks' lads said to him, 'You have ruined your soil structure for years to come and you will get awful drainage problems later.'

In a bit of a temper, Len replied, 'You gardeners make me sick with your technical jargon. The roller did a grand job for me. It was only the weather that let us down.'

Well, the pitch gradually became worse. You just could not get the water to drain away after the heavy rain. After one really heavy downpour, the day before a league match, I went, totally dejected, onto one of the Hamil Road terraces and looked down the Lorne Street side of the pitch. In a straight line there were six pools of water, so evenly spaced that Mother Nature could not have done it. Next, I went over to the Railway Paddock side of the ground and there were two even bigger pools of water lying on the pitch, once again perfectly spaced. I decided there and then what the problem was. The Staffordshire Public Works chairman, who was also a Vale director, had over a period of time dug huge holes (sump holes they called them) in every wet spot on the ground and had filled them with gravel.

The conclusion that I came to (which was later proved to be 100% correct), was that the sump holes had been dropped on top of the main drainage system, thus breaking some pipes in the main drains and these broken pipes had not been replaced. At that particular time, I thought there was nothing I could do. I thought, I'll have to wait until the end of the season, but then I thought, hang on a bit. Test your theory out on those main drains by pushing drainage rods up the mains' pipes and if you come to a full stop near to those very wet areas, you will have proved your point. So, over to the park I went and I borrowed enough drainage rods to go well past the centre of the pitch and certainly more than enough to prove my theory. My rodding points at this time, or so I thought, were accessible through grid holes of 6" diameter, sunk in the red ash path on top of the drains and there I met another problem. I just could not get the drainage rods to go through those grid holes. However, after a little

21

thought, I reasoned that as these drains went through the ash path to the wall I only had to dig up about five metres of track and lift out three drainpipes. That way I could get enough leverage to put the rods in, do my rodding and then replace the pipes. Before commencing the work, however, I talked it over with the ground director and asked him where on earth the plans to the ground were, and, in particular, where the plans to the drainage system of the ground were.

'Mr. Pinfold has them,' he replied, 'and I will get them for you,' which he did after about three days. I opened them up in the secretary's office and the first thing that took my eye was little squares drawn all over the place. I counted them and there were fifty-four.

'What the hell are these red squares?' I asked the ground director.

'Sump holes,' came the reply.

Next, I took a long hard look at the drainage system as shown on the plan. There was nothing wrong there as far as I could see. It consisted of what is called the herringbone system, with main drains going across the pitch and lateral drains going into the mains. On the plan, there was drawn what was described as a mains catchment drain and this was supposed to go the whole length of both terrace walls. This was to get the water from the pitch mains and into that catchment drain by way of a collar pipe, or what is commonly known as an "S" bend.

I dug up the first area on the track, took out three or four pipes, put some of the rods up and, yes, bang on, they came to a halt exactly where one of those wet patches was. Feeling pleased to have found the problem, I decided to go right through to the track wall and ease the collar out, to see if there was a blockage in that drain. The ground director had gone away to Wales for a few days and, as they say, while the cat's away, the mice will play, and there awaiting me was a big shock. The main drain across the perimeter wall, which was shown on the plan, did not exist! The collar pipe, which was fitted to the main pitch drain, went nowhere! It was sitting plum on the ash bed. I then made my first big decision without consulting anyone. I decided that one by one those collars would be taken out and the main drains taken right back to the track wall at the end of each drain. I would then not only have a point at which I could put my rods in, but also the water (which should have gone into the main drain, but did not) would go through the rodding eye and into the concrete. I completed two and had started the third when the ground director came back sooner than expected. I'm sure that someone had been in contact with him and told him to get back quickly because he looked very displeased indeed. However, when I had explained all things to him and shown him my evidence, he was more than happy to let me complete the job. We both called this our rodding eye system thereafter. This work took me right through to the end of the season and it was completed in time for my next big job, the renovation of the pitch.

Three weeks before the end of the season, I had soil delivered and tipped on the ash path. With help from various sources, it was sieved onto the track ready for putting onto the pitch. One week before the end of the season, I had drainpipes and gravel delivered at various points on the ash track to save as much time and work as possible. Just before we started our work on the pitch, Roy Chapman, who was playing for us then, came in to do a bit of training. He stopped, put his hands on his hips and said, 'I've been around in this game some time now, but in all those years I have never seen any bugger work as hard as you, nor have I ever seen a job organised in the way in which you have organised this one. If medals were awarded to groundsmen, yours would be a gold one. You deserve to have the best pitch in the league!'

When we started work on the pitch, I was allowed to hire four Parks' chaps who came to me when they had finished their work in the parks. For one whole week, working until dark, we worked through all those bloody sump holes and replaced all the broken pipes in them. In addition, of course, I was working during the daytime on the pitch. The whole area was over-seeded and all the closed season work was carried out. My efforts even merited an article and a photograph in the "Groundsman's Journal".

I am very happy to state here that since I left, every groundsman who has worked at the Vale has carried on the work of the pitch improvements which I started, especially Bob Fairbanks and Steve Speed. Unfortunately, Bob eventually had to take a less stressful role in the club due to ill health, which was a great pity because he was an excellent groundsman and one hell of a nice fellow.

The pitch greatly improved over the two seasons after my renovation. Unfortunately, what little help I had from inside became less. It was during this period that the ground director came onto the pitch with a letter in his hand. 'A lad from Norton Green,' he said, 'has wrote us a lovely letter enquiring if we need an assistant here, and I think you should go and see him. If he does not want a lot of money, then you can take him on as your permanent assistant, because I am sick of you always moaning about you having no help out here.'

I went down to Norton Green the same day and there was Doug Foster (Terry's brother), a grand lad, sick to death of being unemployed. He had nice parents and was just not bothered about the money side of the job. The ground director spoke to him the next day and we engaged him, and he became the most loyal chap that I had at the club.

I need to say just one final word on the pitch. Whatever work is done there, you will never fully cure the drainage problems during the wet spells because the pitch is on a filled in marl hole. It does not have a subsoil structure, which is so very important to the water table, and I am afraid that short of digging the whole lot up, importing subsoil and completely re-laying the pitch, everyone will just have to grin and bear it during wet spells.

6

The Groundsman's Woes

When I joined the Vale as the groundsman, one thing that stuck out, which had not registered in my mind as a supporter, was the colour of the paint. Everywhere was a very bright green. It was a ghastly colour for a football ground and I talked about this to the ground director. He agreed with me and thought that repainting should be made a priority, with a start to be made during the closed season. It was agreed that I should paint over the green on all the doors and exit gates with black gloss, and the turnstiles with some sort of grey paint. But the ground director told me to go steady and do a bit at a time because of the cost of the paint and brushes.

Well, the paint and brushes cost the club nothing. At that particular time, a firm of industrial painters was there painting the floodlight lamps and pylons, and one day, when I was cutting the grass, the owner of the firm came over to me and introduced himself as Bill Mawman. He was a chap with a broad grin and was a larger than life character. I instantly liked the man so much that I became the gardener at his house in Knypersley. I am still there now almost thirty years after, but sadly Bill has now passed away. I do not know if it was the fact that I was doing Bill's garden or whether it was because he liked me, but whatever it was, in the next few years he saved the Vale hundreds of pounds. First of all, he gave me the black gloss paint and brushes for all the doors, followed by gallons of grey paint, which his firm used to paint the gas storage tanks in various parts of the country, for which he had the contract. He loaned me portable towers, and boards and trestles, and he gave me gallons of white emulsion paint for the toilets. Yes, I could get anything off the man. I only had to ask. My ground director of later years once said to me, 'I have known Bill Mawman for years, but I cannot get a bloody thing out of him and yet you can get anything.'

Well, I think what Bill knew was that I was not asking for myself, but because of my great pride in wanting to see things looking spick and span at the Vale. Or it could have been my approach when I used to go to his factory in Hobson Street, Burslem. I would creep in very quietly, open his office door and yell out, 'Hey up, Bill! Lock away your paint and brushes,

25

and lock up all your gear! That scrounging bugger from Port Vale is here again!' It never failed to produce that big, broad grin right across his face and I never left empty handed—the salt of the earth Bill was to me.

At Vale, I was expected to do many jobs, but there was very little appreciation for whatever I did and this eventually led to arguments between me and the club chairman. This was out of sheer frustration on my part. The first instance was about four days before we were due to play Manchester City in what they termed 'a very prestigious pre-season friendly match'. During that summer, when we had not been working on the pitch, we had spent a lot of time painting the entrance, the players' tunnel, the track wall and the stand wall, besides doing other jobs, and this had led to us getting a little behind with what I had always considered to be my main job, the pitch. A firm of welders had moved on to the Bycars End to carry out much-needed repairs to the crush barriers. At about 10 a.m. on the Tuesday prior to the Manchester City game, the boss of the firm came onto the pitch and he said to me, 'You and your mate have got to go onto the Bycars End, along with my chap, for the next day or two and help him with the welding.'

'No chance!' I said. 'I'm behind now with my pitch.'

'Well, you've got to,' he said, 'the chairman says so.'

'Well, I'm not going to,' I replied.

He disappeared and about five minutes later, he returned with the chairman. 'Leave the pitch,' said the chairman, 'and help with the welding.'

A lengthy argument took place, but I stuck to my guns until eventually I blew my top. 'Oh, piss off and let me get on with my work,' I bellowed at the chairman. Red hot with temper himself by now, he turned and left the pitch, but our friend in charge of the welding work stayed put. 'You wouldn't talk to me like that if I was the chairman,' he said.

I replied, 'You do not know what you are talking about. You do not know what they expect of us out here. If I had one hand tied to a machine, a sweeping brush in the other and a paint brush up my bloody arse they still would not be satisfied!'

His final words at this point were, 'You would not talk to me like that anyway.'

We did not help out with that work, but on the Friday morning, the work having been completed, there again stood our friend. 'Denis,' he said, 'I take back all I said to you on Tuesday. I never thought there was so much work to being a groundsman. I have never seen two chaps work harder than you and your mate and if you were on my staff, you would be

26

the highest paid chaps.'

'Tell that to the chairman,' I replied.

'I already have!' he said.

I was called into the secretary's office at the beginning of June. The secretary said, 'The police have closed the Lorne Street side of the ground because they say that the broken concrete is dangerous. We have had two estimates in, one for £1,000 and one for £750. We simply can't afford that sort of money. If you leave the painting jobs this season, can you do us a temporary job, thus enabling us to open up that area in a few weeks' time?'

'We will do our best,' I said, and we did that job, only for me to be called into the secretary's office one morning and Arthur McPherson, a director, was in there.

'We've had a bill for sand, gravel and cement,' said Norman Jones, 'and the amount of cement you have used seems excessive.'

Arthur chipped in, 'It does indeed!'

He gave the bill to me to look at and it was a grand total of £39! 'What the sodding hell do you want?' I roared. 'That bill is bloody peanuts and yet you still aren't satisfied. Don't ask me to do any more jobs here because I won't.'

Later that morning, Arthur McPherson came out to me and apologised and said, 'I should not have listened to the secretary.'

'Those offices, the boardroom and those other areas look a right mess,' Mr. Singer, a director, said one morning. 'Do you think you can put a bit of paint on when you have got no match during the season?'

'We'll do our best,' I replied.

The passage, the entrance hall and the dressing rooms were always done during the closed season by the trainer, Lol Hamlett, his assistant Bill Cope and the groundstaff boys. We did the two secretaries' offices, the manager's offices, the ladies' room, the players' wives' room and the boardroom. Everywhere was beginning to look lovely when once again there was a familiar cry: 'It's costing a lot of money for paint and brushes, this job is, Denis. It's cost us £69 up till now. How much more do you reckon you are going to spend?'

'£69!' I replied in total disgust. 'You just try to get anyone in for that amount to do what we have just done!'

About three days later, Mr. Singer said, 'There's one place you have missed, the directors' toilet. It's filthy!'

'We're too busy this week,' I replied.

'Well, I want it done for next week's match,' he said.

Well, we did it. Oh yes, we did it alright—daffodil yellow! Imagine that at a football ground, if you will. There was a complete outcry from all who went on that toilet: 'Put any colour on top of that which you have got. For God's sake get it done!' Well, on top of yellow, we painted it grey and every brushful of paint we put on, we did with a bloody big grin on our faces. We really did enjoy winding those soft buggers up!

I reckon the water main was probably the biggest job that we tackled.

'Our water bills are dreadful,' said the chairman one day. 'The secretary has rung our neighbours, Stoke and Crewe, and our bills are above fifty percent more than theirs. Well, you know we've been told by the meter reader that we've got a burst and we have even been threatened with an enforcement order to make us repair it, but we do not have any money at all to do anything like that.'

So, we had to turn the water off after every match, including that which fed all the toilet blocks, and we only put it on one hour before kickoff. Months afterwards, they were still complaining about the size of the bills and at this point we got the water board to come in and try to pinpoint where the burst was. After checking it, they informed us that the problem lay somewhere between the main gates to the Railway Paddock and the main gates at the far end of the Railway Stand.

'How much will the work cost?' the secretary asked the water board chap.

'Someone else will have to come up and answer that question,' he answered and the next day another bloke came to give us a price.

'£500!' said Mr. Singer. 'There's no way we can afford that.'

'Well, if you can do your own digging it will drastically reduce the cost,' the chap said and he then left us to think it over.

Once again the familiar question was asked: 'Denis, do you think you and Doug can do the digging for us? There's no match until a week on Saturday.'

I replied, 'We'll have a go for you.'

The digging at first was in solid yellow, sticky clay and at this point I wondered if I had done the right thing in agreeing to tackle such a big job. However, after days of digging, we hit solid black ash and it took us about four days before we found the problem. The copper pipe was decayed in places due to the fact that it had been laid in black ash in which there was a lot of rough pieces. Due to top ground pressure, these had pierced the pipe in so many places, you could not have counted the holes. We removed the whole length of the copper pipe from the Railway Paddock main gates, right down to the exit gates at the far end of the stand. We then put into the bottom of the trench six inches of sand, which we had to carry in buckets because you could not push a barrow anywhere near, so rough was the ground. Next, we called in a local plumbing firm and rolled PVC pipe the whole length of the trench. The plumber connected it up at both ends and Doug and I put another six inches of sand on top of the pipe and finished off by backfilling the trench with ash. In total, we used 10 tonnes of sand, which was free courtesy of a very good friend of the club and we paid £35 for the roll of piping fitted by the plumber.

Month after month went by and no-one said anything to us until one day, Norman Jones remarked, 'Denis, that job you and Doug did on the water mains is saving us hundreds of pounds. Our water bills are now less than half what they were.'

'Great,' I replied.

Now, the ground director, Len Cliff, was in those days living in the Isle of Man and only came over for some of the first team games. When he did so, his first job was to go through all of the bills with the secretary. It was during one of these visits that he asked me about jobs that I had done and he seemed a little annoyed on this occasion. He asked, 'You haven't replaced those broken sheets on the stand roof have you?'

'No,' I replied.

'Christ,' he retorted. 'It's going to rain this afternoon and we'll have everyone complaining.'

'Well,' I said, 'I fetched the new sheets last week and they're in my shed. I attempted to do the job last week. I put the ladders up and then put cat boards onto the roof, but as I tried to remove the first sheet, the boards moved and I was lucky not to have had a very nasty accident. But of course,' I continued, 'I was not keen in the first place. You see I do not like heights.'

'Well, you soft sod, you should have had more sense in the first place,' he said and with that he stalked off.

As I went about my pre-match tasks, I began to think about the ground director. I thought, he's been out here complaining about the jobs I haven't done, but he never said a word about the water main and when I next caught sight of him I said, 'The water bills are a lot better, aren't they Mr. Cliff?'

He very curtly replied, 'Oh yes.'

I was gutted at such a lack of appreciation for such a big job and my next thought was, right you bastard, I was going to spend the money I had made from the copper pipe on brushes and paint for the ground next summer, but instead I will share the £60 with Doug, and that is exactly what I did. I have never had any regrets having done so. This episode upset me even more because when the piping had been removed from the trench my one and only thought was about how much money I could make in order to buy paint and brushes for the summer painting programme.

I made four journeys to the local scrapyard in my own car and I put into an envelope the £60 I had made on the piping. I placed it under the mattress which we slept on at home, in case we had a break-in, to make sure that the Vale's money was not taken and it remained there for many weeks until the ground director's show of complete indifference to all the work that Doug and I had put into that job.

7

Expulsion From The League

In all the time that I worked at the Vale, the worst period was when we were expelled from the league and had a heavy fine clapped on us to boot. This was after an inquiry into the signing of a lad who was under age and should have still been at school. The lad in question was a Geordie by the name of Trevor Finnigan. Sir Stanley Matthews, the manager, took the blame for this, which, in my opinion, was ridiculous. The secretary at a football club is the man who is, or should be, primed in the laws of the game and the chairman should also have known better than Sir Stanley what the score was. However, they probably thought that because of Sir Stanley's standing in the game, they would get away with it, but, of course, they did not.

The club was in a very depressed state indeed, leading up to the inquiry, and to me, as a lifelong fan of the club, it was unthinkable that there would be no Port Vale if things went against the club. However, thank goodness, they did not, but what fun we had on the day that the decision was announced. Sir Stanley was always at the ground early every morning, even though he travelled from his home in Blackpool. Ann, our lady of many jobs, was always there shortly afterwards and I was not far behind. We had been told the day before that the decision would be conveyed to us the next day and as I went through the glass doors, Sir Stanley came out of his office. He said, 'Come in a minute, Denis,' and he explained to me what the decision was. Apart from the fine, he told me that we would, at the end of the season, be expelled from the league and would have to apply for re-election, just as the bottom four did in those days. Anyway, he told me not to worry because they had been promised total support by the Football League club chairmen. (In the event, we were readmitted by 39 votes to 9). Sir Stanley concluded our conversation by saying that there was to be a press conference at 10.45 that morning to explain what was what, but he forgot to ask me to say nothing to the reporters.

This was where the fun started. The media men arrived early to try to be first to the story, but they were getting no joy from the people inside. I had just started to spike the pitch at about 9.30 when out came a stocky little chap. He came right over to me and said, with a hint of great gloating in his voice, 'In some ways, it's a great tragedy to see the club thrown out of the league, but it serves them right anyway. But never mind, they will be able to build houses on here now the club is dead.'

'Well,' I said, 'you are wrong there, mate. Someone here will find the money to pay the fine and we will get re-elected in the summer.'

Anyway, he turned away from me and I have never seen anyone run so fast. Within ten minutes, all hell broke loose inside the club. Unintentionally I had really put the cat amongst the pigeons. Some of those people from the media were behaving like hooligans and could not wait for the press conference. At about midday, I was asked by the secretary to unlock a gate on the Bycars End. I was not told what for, nor did I bother to ask and I did not find out until I went in for my lunch break. 'You can lock the gate now,' I was told. 'Sir Stanley has left.' I was told that a very good friend of Sir Stanley had parked his car down the path by the Bycars End and had shepherded him there and got him away from the ranting and raving mob of media men. I did not blame Sir Stanley for that. He is a very shy man, who throughout his career had let his feet do the talking for him, and I think some of those clowns from the media would have made mincemeat out of him.

During the afternoon, most of the media men left, but there were a few who hung about like vultures, and it was then that I and the club had the last laugh, at their expense. At about 4.45, out came the same little chap who had gleaned the information from me earlier that morning.

'Do you always work this late?' he asked.

'Oh, yes,' I replied, 'and I shall be working later still from now on because I have got to get this lot ready for our promotion push next season.' I was gloating.

'What time does Sir Stanley leave the ground?' he asked.

That question was music to my ears and, with great pleasure and a huge grin, I replied, 'Oh, he left about midday.'

'Oh no, he did not,' our reporter friend said, 'because I have never left that front entrance all day.'

'Well, he left by the back entrance at midday,' I replied.

The reporter was sick as a bloody parrot, but he gave me a final glance before leaving the pitch.

8

The Lighter Side Of Football

Football has its funny side and I would like to think that I gave the folks working at the Vale as many laughs as they gave to me. I would hate to be remembered as 'that miserable sod who worked outside'!

Footballers are buggers for taking the mickey and one Friday morning, while they were jogging around the track, about three of them stopped. Ray Williams, the biggest mickey-taker of the lot, much to the amusement of the other two, asked me, 'Hey, Den, are you going to cut the grass today?'

I replied, 'I am not, Ray. You see, the way you lot are playing at present, come quarter to five tomorrow afternoon you will need somewhere to hide and even then I don't know whether the grass will be long enough to hide you!' I never heard him mention the grass again.

The next laugh was the heavy roller saga. When results were going against us, it was always the pitch that was to blame and in the case of some of the players, it was always the roller. They would pass their opinion to one player in particular whom they knew would always shoot their bullets for them, Tommy McLaren. 'Heavy roller, pal, for Saturday's match?' was always his question. Now, we had made by a blacksmith, some two years previously, two four-foot-long rollers of exactly the same weight, but we only ever used one of them because the handle of the other was four inches in diameter, which was far too big to get your hands around. I stood looking at the unused roller one day and a very good idea struck me. I gave Doug, my assistant, £1 and asked him to go to the shop and fetch me a small tin of white paint and a two-inch paint brush. When he arrived back, I got a wire brush, cleaned all the muck off the handles of the rollers and on one of them I painted '$\frac{1}{2}$ cwt.'. On the other roller, I painted '3 cwt.'. I then said to Doug, 'On Fridays, before the first team games, we'll put the $\frac{1}{2}$ cwt. roller at the corner of the pitch and we will pull the 3 cwt. one around the track just as the players are coming out to do a bit of training. And, as we do so, we'll puff and pant like hell and make it look like real hard work and when the moaners are within earshot of us, we'll mutter and swear at having to use a heavy roller for their benefit. Then, before they disappear to finish their workout, we'll pull it across the pitch a time or two, going through the same motions.'

Well, the first time we did this little exercise, we won the match on the Saturday 3-1. Like parrots they were on the Monday after the match: 'We were right. We told you it wanted a heavy roller. The surface was brilliant on Saturday, much better with that roller you used on Friday.'

This was exactly the same weight roller that we had always used, so that killed the heavy roller argument forever!

At the end of January 1972, the Vale played Bournemouth at home and we had by then played numerous times so that the middle of the pitch was bare of grass (as you would expect in those circumstances). About two hours before the kickoff, their manager, John Bond, and his assistant came out. They paraded all over the pitch and up and down the middle, and, as they came across to where I was, all I could hear was, 'The wings are beautiful, but the middle is a total disgrace.' They then stopped and asked me, 'What on earth is up with the middle of your pitch? There is no grass on it. It's all bumpy and not at all suitable for good football. The whole of our pitch has got a lovely covering of grass on it.'

'And I should think so too,' I replied. 'Your ground is in one of the best parts of the country where you get very little frost, if any at all. The further you come north, the harder it is to keep the grass on the whole of the pitch for the whole of the season.' I concluded at that point and Mr. Bond offered no argument and left.

The following season, the Bournemouth fixture was at the beginning of November. Again out came Mr. Bond and his assistant to inspect the pitch. This time, he came over to where I was working and said, 'What a transformation! It's beautiful—it's a credit to you. Much different to when we were here last season, perfect for good football. Have you got rid of that clown who was here last season?'

Now, if you show a bull a red rag, be prepared to run and if you criticize and talk to a groundsman in this way, you will not get bulled out, but you sure as hell will get a right earful. I looked at the cocky little sod standing there, with a cigar in his gob. It was as big as a telegraph pole and you could have flown our club flag on the end of it. He was dressed like a tailor's dummy and talked like a "pox doctor's clerk". Because he had made such an ass of himself, he was at my mercy. I looked at him and, with a great big grin on my face, took off the hat which I was wearing, but had not worn on my previous meeting. 'Take a good, long, hard look at me Mr. Bond,' I said, 'because you are looking at the same clown who was here last season. If there is a clown out here, it is not me!

34

You manage your football team and I will manage my ground. Now piss off and leave me alone.'

'I'll report you up there,' he said, pointing to the directors' box.

Much later in the morning, he came out again, but this time was much friendlier. He offered me a cigar, which I politely refused because I do not smoke.

Another very similar incident occurred when we were at home to Wrexham on a Monday night and again there was very little grass around the middle of the pitch. About four of the visiting party came onto the pitch and there was a big 6 foot chap airing his views. The others were listening to him in complete awe and one of his ideas was to spread a good load of builders' sand over the middle. He also suggested covering the whole pitch in winter with straw, covering it in farmyard manure in the closed season and, most incredibly, dressing the whole middle in charcoal. Now, I have never heard such a load of rubbish and at this point he tried to involve me. I thought he was the manager and said, 'Well, you bloody managers are all the same. All that you people ever do is use the pitch as an excuse. You want to sod off and do your own job!'

At that point, he flew into an awful rage and roared, 'You jumped up, hairy-arsed git of a groundsman! Don't stand there mouthing off at me. I'll knock your bloody head off!'

I did not argue with him because he was much too big and nasty for me. About fifteen minutes later, out came a very dapper and well-spoken little chap. We had a chat about various things, during which I said, 'Their manager has just been out moaning, and me and him have had a right old ding-dong. And he even threatened to top me if I did not shut my trap.'

With a long grin on his face, he informed me, 'He's not the manager. I am!' He put his hand out and introduced himself: 'John Neal,' he said. He later went on to manage Chelsea and he concluded our chat by saying, 'He's only the club reporter, he is. He knows nothing about football pitches, but he can be a right nasty chap sometimes because he is very quick-tempered!'

One afternoon, Lol Hamlett came into the boot room with a small empty whisky bottle in his hand and said, 'Some of the lads like a mouthful of whisky before they go onto the field for a match. Just look at the size of that bottle, Den. No fizzing use at all if Tommy McLaren gets his mouth around that! There'll be nothing left for anyone else. They're a mean lot of devils, these directors of ours.'

At that point, he disappeared taking with him the empty whisky bottle.

Now, Lol did not realise that all the backroom staff and I knew that he had one bottle supplied by the club and another which he filled up himself by creeping into where the directors' supply was kept. He would fill up his bottle and top up the directors' bottle with water or cold tea, to make it appear that none had gone. One Saturday, I was outside, talking to one of the police officers, when out came Mr. Cliff.

'Denis,' he said. 'Do you know who is tampering with the whisky?'

'Not me,' I said, 'I don't touch the stuff.'

'Well, someone is!' Mr. Cliff said. 'Fred Pinfold has just poured himself a glass and one for the visiting chairman. He has spat his out all over the boardroom floor and he is bloody livid! I have just sent one of the lads out to get a new bottle from the off-licence.'

He mentioned one or two possibilities as to what was happening, but finished off by saying, 'One thing for certain. It's not Lol Hamlett because he is teetotal.' At that point, he left.

Now, for quite some time after that, everyone in the back room staff, me included, was under suspicion—that is everyone except Lol, and I find it strange that a man of his standing did not come clean because, after all, he was not taking the stuff for himself!

One of the biggest laughs of all concerned our new floodlights. They were much more powerful than those they had replaced. We were due to play on a Monday night. During the weekend, we had a heavy snowfall and by the Monday morning, there were five to six inches of snow on the pitch and no chance of us playing whatever we tried to do. At about 10.45, the ground director, Len Cliff, stood hands in pockets looking thoughtfully across the ground. 'I say,' he said, 'I am only a layman in these matters so to speak, but as these floodlights are much more powerful than those they have replaced, do you think that if you switched them on now that they would melt . . . '

He stopped abruptly because he must have caught the look on my face. 'I'm off,' he blurted out and, as he did so, I remarked, 'Bring some bacon and eggs up and we'll have a fry up in the centre circle!'

The secretary and chairman were always moaning about kids sneaking into the ground on match days and not paying. If I had been in their shoes, with the team playing so badly, I would have been more concerned about those leaving early. I was sick to death of the continuous moaning and I was talking one day to a local gardener, when he made a suggestion. He said it would stop the little sods forever if some waste oil and bitumen was put into a large bucket and mixed with pig shit—and then spread on top of the wall. He said, 'It will make a mess on their hands and will leave a bloody stink. It will keep them away forever.'

As I mixed it in the bucket, it really did stink! I went to our worst sneak-in spot, at the Bycars End, and put the mixture right along the top of the wall just before midday on the morning of the first team fixture versus Preston North End. At about two o'clock that afternoon, which was the usual time when the kids started to sneak in, I made my way down to the Bycars End and hid myself away inside a turnstile shed. I did not have to wait very long before I heard the voices of giggling girls right where I had daubed that awful stuff.

'You go in first,' I heard one of them say, and I then positioned myself in a spot where I could see them, but they could not see me. Over came the first pair of hands, right slap bang into that awful stuff.

'Christ Almighty!' the poor little bugger shrieked, as her hands disappeared. 'Christ Almighty! The dirty swines—the dirty bastards have put something on top of the wall! Just look at my hands! Yuk, what a bloody stink!'

She then made her way to the exit gates, which were, in those days, made up of metal bars, and she raked her hands over the bars to try and scrape them clean, and all the time she was yelling to the other girls, 'The dirty, lousy swines! My hands will be ruined after this. The dirty bastards!'

As she moved away from the gates, she gave them a good kick and shouted to the other girls, 'When they have all gone home tonight, and it's pitch-black, I am coming back and I will kick every fucking gate down on the Bycars End.' And to emphasise her point she yelled, 'I fucking well will! Honest, I fucking well will!'

Whenever we used any of the stuff afterwards, we always referred to it as 'our dirty, black, bastard swine'!

During one closed season, I was having terrible trouble with pigeons coming onto the pitch and nicking the seed, leaving big, bare patches. What I did to scare them off was to bang together two empty one gallon oil drums, to make as much noise as possible. When I was doing this one day, the "pig shit" gardener, who had a nearby allotment, wandered into the ground.

'Bloody sick to death of these thieving pigeons,' I said to him.

'Oh,' he replied, 'I can get rid of them for you and it will not cost you a penny. I will come across tomorrow at about two o'clock.'

There he was as promised, the next day, with a biscuit tin in his hand

and a bottle under his arm. Before I could ask him what the contents of the tin and the bottle were, he shook the tin and said, 'Rice, just like your mother used to put in the pudding.' He then put the bottle down and said, 'Whisky, that is.' He removed the top from the rice tin and into it he poured the whisky. After he had allowed a period of time to elapse for the soaking of the rice, he went onto the pitch and scattered it. We both sat on the trainer's bench, at the side of the pitch, and down came the pigeons. They had a whale of a time!

'What do we do now?' I asked him.

'Be patient for a while,' he replied and after about half an hour, he got up to go onto the pitch. As he approached the little group of pigeons, they hardly moved and he picked up the first one, stretched its neck and threw it down on the ground dead. On to the next one he went and did the same, and as he was about to pick up the third one, I shouted, 'Hey, bloody hell, hang on a minute. I did not bargain for this. It's bloody murder it is!'

He ignored me and, as I made my way towards him, he had about five or six of the poor little sods lying there dead. With a twinkle in his eye, he turned to me and asked, 'What did you think I was going to do? Give them a good feed, pat them on the head and ask them not to be silly little buggers and in future leave your seed alone?' And, pointing to ten dead birds, he concluded, 'Them buggers won't give you any more trouble!'

Many people have said nasty things about Len Parton, the groundsman, from time to time, but I reckon that he was a damned good servant to the Vale and one hell of a nice chap. He was one of the most likeable fellows that I have ever met out of all I knew at the Vale, he gave seventeen years' loyal service and he was more than the groundsman. He looked after all the turnstile men on match days and this was during the time when we were drawing really big crowds. He was the social club steward and did a lot of work organising the Vale's original sweep.

I received a message one day from my superintendent when I worked for the Parks Department, asking me to go over right away to see Len as he had problems with his mowing machine and he had to cut the pitch for the match which was to take place that night. I took my little bag of tools with me and nipped over to the ground. There he was, on the ash path, arguing the toss with the manager, Freddie Steele. The Vale were playing Carlisle United that night in their second home fixture of the 1964-1965 season and the manager was adamant that Len had got to cut the grass before kickoff because he said it was too long.

Len greeted me with a smile and said, 'My bloody mower has packed in again. How can I cut grass without a mower? It doesn't need cutting anyway.'

Without getting involved in the argument, I went over to where the mower was standing, took out the spark plug and replaced it with a new one, and with the first pull of the starting rope it started. Len climbed onto the seat of the mower and away he went. After he had been up and down four or five times, the lines on the grass looked great, like you see in farmers' fields in spring when they are rolling or harrowing, but there was one problem—as far as I could see, no grass was going up into the grass box, but I dared not say anything. I thought, he'll blow my bloody head off if I open my mouth. Eventually, he stopped the machine, got off the seat and asked the manager. 'Will that do for you then, boss?'

'Yes,' replied Fred, 'but I want it all done exactly like that before kickoff.' At that point, the manager left, but I stayed behind to have a word with Len.

'Len,' I said, 'how the hell have you managed to pull that one? You know and I know and I would have thought he would have known that the grass hasn't been cut.'

With an impish grin on his face, he replied, 'Thicker than pig shit some of these buggers are here, but it just shows that I was right in the first place when I said that the grass did not need cutting.'

I replied as I left, 'Well, I still don't know how the hell you managed to get away with that one.'

The result of that match, much to Len's amusement, was a 3-1 defeat! The next day, he said to me, 'It did not trouble the visitors, did it? They showed us how to play!'

I was in Len's office one morning, paying him my sweep money, and we were talking about various subjects relevant to the ground. In walked one of the groundstaff lads.

'Len,' he said, 'there's a hole just outside one of these main gates.'

Len gave him a really wicked look and snarled at him, 'What the bloody hell do you want me to do about it? Go and get a barrow, go behind the Railway Stand and get some of that black ash and fill the hole in!'

'But Len,' the lad butted in. 'But Len, but Len,' he yelled.

Len picked up an empty cardboard box and threw it at the lad, shouting, 'Sod off and do as you are told, and don't try winding me up first thing in the morning!' As he left, there was Len chuntering to himself, 'Bloody groundstaff lads, no use at all they aren't. Only thing they're fit for is kicking a bloody ball about!'

At that point, I turned and left his office and was on my way out through the gates and there stood the lad, looking completely bewildered, looking into the hole.

'Bloody hell, son,' I shouted. 'Come away from there. That's a pit shaft!'

I dashed back into Len's office and said, 'Len, you'd better have a look straight away at that lot. It's a pit shaft, not a hole.'

Out he went to have a look and when he saw it, he flew into an awful rage. 'You stupid little sod,' he shouted at the lad. 'You can't fill that with a barrow! Have you got no sense at all? That's a bloody pit shaft! Don't you know the difference?'

Now, if that lad had looked completely bewildered before, he now looked absolutely stunned.

'Stop where you are,' Len said to the lad, 'and don't let anyone go anywhere near that hole. I'll get the chairman down.' And he walked away, chuntering even louder now, 'Stupid, thick sods, groundstaff lads! Who wants them?'

From time to time everyone gets bored with their daily routine and groundsmen at football clubs are no different from other workers. At football clubs, when things are going wrong on the field, life gets very tense indeed for everyone. During such spells, I relieved my boredom by playing silly little games with the junior pros. One day, after I had ragged one of them to death by telling him that he was slower than my granny, he retorted by saying, 'I could give you ten yards in one hundred yards and still beat you, you bloody old git!'

'Right, tomorrow dinner time,' I replied and there he was, right on time, with his mates to cheer him on. It was no problem at all for him as he surged past me, leaving me breathless and knackered.

'We'll have another do tomorrow,' I said, 'but this time, it will be a handicap race. There will be no yards start. I will run in my boots and you will have a Wellington boot on one foot and a football boot on the other.' There we were again—exactly the same result and now the cheeky little sod was really taking the sap.

'One more race, tomorrow dinner time,' I said, 'and for this one, I will put football boots on and you can have a plimsole on one foot and a Wellington boot on the other. And in one hand, you can carry one of those five-pound weights which you do your training with.'

There we were again, but this time running shoulder to shoulder.

Halfway down the ash track, his face was as red as fire, his eyes were as big as golf balls and he was panting like an old horse. Well, I could hardly run for laughing, but, as I began to gain ground, he panicked and dropped the weight. He shouted, 'Stuff you, I am not carrying that,' but, unfortunately for him, the weight got caught up in his feet and sent him crashing onto the grass track. I can see him now, lying there, grunting out the words, 'Sod you! We are only having proper races in the future!'

But whatever you did on any of those lads, they always took it in good part and always got even in one way or another. Never more so than when I was having a lovely shower and they would come creeping up behind me, and wham, a big bucket of cold water would hit me in the back! This trick really backfired on them one day, when it was not me using the shower, but the great man himself, Sir Stanley, who was showering off! The other trick they had was to grease the door handles, which were round in shape, and really took some turning after they had greased them.

One day after a cup tie, there was litter lying all over the place and all the staff were down in the mouth because we had lost. Nevertheless, we did what I consider to be the daftest trick of all. We had a lovely big fire at the back of the stand, with all the plastic cups and hot dog wrappers, which we had collected. There seemed to be no end to the litter lying about and, to put it mildly, I was bloody sick of seeing it. Doug and I took two big sacks full and put them on the fire. As I stood back, I spotted three empty five-gallon drums, which had contained bitumen that we had used to paint areas of the ground.

'Grab one of those, Doug,' I said, and this he did. I hammered the top down, to make it airtight, and placed it on the fire, hoping to create a bit of a bang, but I never expected to see what I did as it began to swell in the heat.

I said to Doug, 'Let's retreat to the top of the ramp, near the stand, where it will be a bit safer.'

What a good job we did. Boom, bang! It shot up in the air, higher than the stand, and, as it did so, it burst into a great ball of flame.

'Christ, Doug,' I said, 'that is one daft trick too many. We could have been badly injured.'

As we turned to walk away, the fire engine surged up from the depot in Hamil Road and coming round the track was Norman Jones.

'What's happened, lads?' he asked.

'Oh,' I said, 'we are burning the litter round the back of the stand and

41

some of the lads, who are on holiday from school, must have got in through one of the gates. They must have stuck one of those bitumen drums onto our fire. Bloody lucky, we are, that we have not been hurt.'

'Yes, you are!' the firemen said. 'In future keep the gates closed and shift those other drums!'

1. Part of the site of the OLD RECREATION GROUND, HANLEY.

2. MY FATHER, STEPHEN DAWSON, THE VALE CHEERLEADER.

4. KEN GRIFFITHS.

3. COLIN ASKEY.

5. STAN TURNER.

6. PORT VALE, 1950.

7. *The players and officials eagerly awaiting news of the F.A. CUP DRAW IN 1954.*

8. VALE'S F.A. CUP TEAM OF 1954 v. BLACKPOOL:
Back Row: Stan Turner, Albert Mullard, Roy Sproson, Ray King, Basil Hayward, Reg Potts.
Front Row: Colin Askey, Ken Griffiths, Tom Cheadle, Dickie Cunliffe, Albert Leake.

10. TERRY MILES.

9. HARRY POOLE.

11. *PORT VALE, 1957.*

12. KEN HANCOCK.

13. MY ARRIVAL AT THE VALE AS THE GROUNDSMAN, 15 JUNE 1966:
Jackie Mudie (player-manager), John Bostock (groundstaff), me, John Hulme (groundstaff),
Malcolm Carter (groundstaff).

14. PHIL AND ROY SPROSON.

16. *BILL DEARDEN.*

15. *JOHN RUDGE.*

18. *CAROL BRUNDRETT.*

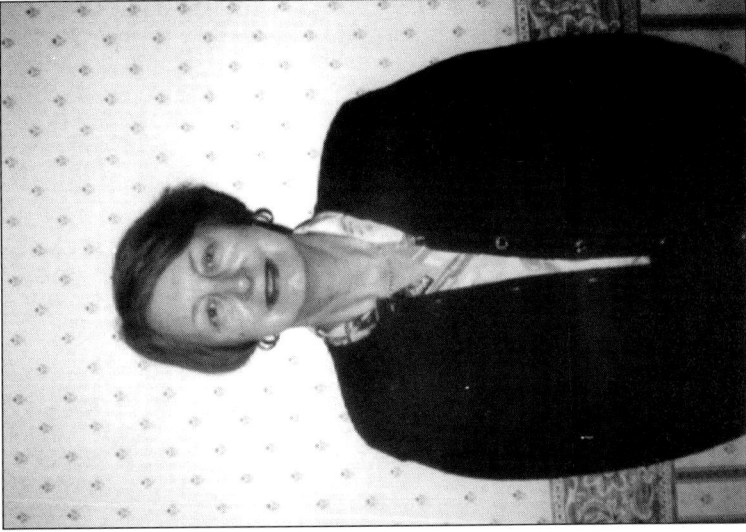

17. *BILL LODEY.*

20. RICK CARTER.

19. MARK GREW.

22. NEIL ASPIN.

21. STEVE SPEED.

24. ESTELLE BAGGLEY.

23. MARTIN FOYLE.

26. JAYNE PATTISON.

25. MICHELLE DOVE.

27. *PORT VALE, 1996-1997: The squad which equalled the club's highest league position since 1931.*

28. MY RETURN TO THE PITCH AT VALE PARK FOR A PHOTO SHOOT IN 1997.

9

Groundsman's Glory!

How do groundsmen, or players for that matter, rate in the board-rooms of football clubs? Not very highly, I'm sorry to say, and I will list one or two examples to show why I have that opinion. I went one Friday morning to collect my wages from the secretary's office and as I entered the room, the chairman was there. The secretary piped up, 'I saw your photograph in the "Sentinel" last night, collecting a groundsman's certificate. I did not think they had certificates for your job.'

'Nor did I,' quipped the chairman.

'Well, you know now, don't you?' I replied. 'And, as a matter of fact, I've got three more to go with that one. That particular certificate is the National Certificate in the Science and Practice of Turf Culture and Sports Ground Management.'

At that point, I left wondering, do these buggers think my job is one for a bloody noddy?

On 27 November 1972, I was expecting a phone call at any time during the day. My wife had gone into the City General Hospital to give birth to our third child and, because I knew that I would be missing for a couple of hours, I kicked in at the ground earlier than usual that morning. Also, we had a reserve match that night, kickoff at 7.45. The weather was great, the pitch was in excellent order and at eleven in the morning it was marked out. The corner flags were put out and the goal nets were put on. Everything, therefore, was in perfect order when my phone call came at 3.30. I went off to the hospital, leaving Doug in charge in case there were any problems and I could not get back in time for the kickoff. After looking at our new arrival and having a kiss and cuddle with my wife, I proudly dashed home to tell the good news to the rest of my family. Then I went back to the ground and arrived there at a quarter to six. In the main entrance hall to the ground stood the chairman and I could tell by his facial expression that he was not very pleased.

'I've been out there looking for you, Denis. Have you been out somewhere?' enquired the chairman.

As proud as punch, I replied, 'The wife has presented me with a lovely little daughter this afternoon and I have been up to the hospital to see them both.'

'Well,' he said, in a very surly voice, 'you do not normally leave the ground until about five when there is a match. I know you go home at that time to have your tea, but going away earlier I'm a bit surprised at because there could be problems.'

Feeling a little deflated, I was turning to go outside when through those same doors burst Ray Williams, one of our players, beaming all over. With his hands in the air, he proudly announced, 'The wife has had a little girl.' Those same two people who had brushed me aside, that is the chairman and the secretary, could not get to him quickly enough!

'Congratulations, Ray,' they said. 'We're so pleased for you. What are you going to have her named?'

They almost kissed his bloody boots!

'I've never seen your wife here,' Mr. Cliff said one day.

'Where would she go if she came?' I asked.

'Well, of course, in there,' he said, pointing to a room marked "Players' Wives' Room". He had taken the bait which my question had intended.

'Well, my wife,' I said, 'is not interested in football, but, even if she was, I will show you why I would never bring her here.'

He looked rather puzzled as he stood there.

'Just follow me, Mr. Cliff,' I said, and he did so. A little distance from the first room was another room and over that door was a sign which said "Ladies' Room". I pointed to the sign and said, 'My wife and the wives of the players are just as much ladies as those of the directors!'

'The players never bother,' he retorted.

'Well,' I concluded, 'let the players look after their own wives, but neither you nor any other director at this club will ever slight my wife!'

I went into the ground one morning and Lol Hamlett met me with the words, 'I've got some awful news, Den. John Nicholson has died as a result of that car accident. It's a real tragedy. Fizzing great bloke, John was.'

Later that morning, I collected the club flag from where we kept it in order to put it onto the flagpole at half-mast. Before I did so, I thought I had better clear it with Mr. Singer who was in the secretary's office. It was a good job that I did! I walked in with the flag held forward and said, 'I take it for granted that with the sad death of John Nicholson, the flag has to go up at half-mast.'

'It is a good job indeed that you have enquired first,' Mr. Singer said, 'because it most certainly does not go up. That flag is only flown at half-mast for officials at this club and only when I give instructions.'

I turned to leave and, as I did so, I said, 'We are ever likely to be a bloody lowly club if that is the way you think about your staff.'

Three years later, Mr. Burgess, a former chairman and a director of long standing, passed away.

'Denis,' Mr. Singer shouted, from the secretary's office, as I passed by. 'Have you got a minute?'

I entered the office and he said to me, 'Denis you know Mr. Burgess has passed away, don't you?'

'Yes,' I replied.

'Well,' he said, 'I want you to put the flag up at half-mast right away.'

'No bloody chance,' I replied. 'You told me some time ago, when I was going to put it up for John Nicholson, that I was not to do so, and I do not care who dies in this club from now on, you will never get me to put that flag up for any of them! And I don't give a sod if you sack me now, on the spot, I'll still not put it up!'

I did not, but someone else did and he also took it down.

Mr. Burgess' funeral was arranged for a Friday afternoon. No-one told me about this, possibly because of the flag episode. The first I knew about this was at 10.00 a.m. on the said Friday and this led me into further hassle.

For weeks previously, various people had pestered me to death to replace three broken windowpanes, two in the player's tunnel and one in the gents' toilet. They had issued me with an instruction that, whatever else I had to leave, these windows must be in for the following Saturday's match. I had ordered the glass and putty from a little shop on Hamil Road and I collected it after my lunch break on the Friday of the funeral. As I went through the front door, with the glass and putty in hand, at 1.30, the secretary shouted from his office, 'Who's that?'

'It's me,' I replied and went into his office with the materials under my arm.

'Where are you going with that lot?' he asked.

'The broken windows,' I replied. 'They're getting right nasty because I haven't done them sooner.'

'You are not doing anything,' he said. 'This ground is closed from two o'clock today. You know it's Mr. Burgess' funeral. Well, surely you are going, aren't you?'

'Well, I only found out at 10.00 today that it was the funeral, but it

45

would not have made any difference to me if I had known earlier,' I said. 'You see, Norman, in all the time that I have been here, he is the only director on Saturday afternoons who has passed me by and totally ignored me, and therefore I am not going to be a hypocrite. When I leave this earth, Norman, I hope that only the folks that I have respected in this life will attend my funeral. I'll bloody well come back and haunt those who come to my funeral who have not respected me. I hate hypocrisy.'

'You will be in real trouble with the directors,' Norman said. 'I would not like to be in your shoes tomorrow, for anything.'

However, it was 5.30 on Friday afternoon before I finished my glazing and I did not receive a reprimand from anyone.

The chairman, Arthur McPherson, had a few words with me before the next home match on the Saturday and, when I explained my points of view to him, his final comments to me were, 'While I do not agree with you on this occasion, because Fred Burgess has been a great servant, I do admire you for having the guts to stick to your principles. I wish there were more in the club like you!'

10

The Contract

The relations between the chairman, Mr. Singer, and me were getting more and more strained every week. He was a very greedy man who just did not seem to know or care about me and Doug. He wanted us to paint this, paint that, put a few nails here, put a few nails there and I could go on and on.

He said, 'During the closed season, I want the crush barriers on the Hamil End painting and the toilets did not have any paint on them last year, so I'll want those done also.'

And my mate Doug and I were soft enough to try and do all these jobs, but things came to a head in the middle of the winter months of 1972-1973. Doug was off sick with a septic throat and, as usual, I could not get any help from inside. The answer, whenever I asked for any, was, 'You've got an assistant out there now.'

However, late one cold Thursday afternoon, I was hand-forking in the Hamil End goalmouth when out came the chairman.

'Leave what you are doing now,' he said. 'I have got a very dirty job for you to do and it's got to be done before the social club opens tonight. I want you to go up to the club and unblock the ladies' toilet. I asked the cleaners to do it this morning, but they have refused flat and I do not blame them one bit. It's a filthy, vile job.'

I straightened up, put the fork in the ground and looked him straight in the face. I was raging inside and battling to control my temper.

'You know,' I said, 'how hard it's been for me this week with Doug off sick and I think I have done pretty well to get the pitch into shape for Saturday's match—and you have the bloody cheek to stand there and tell me that the people you pay to do the cleaning have refused to do it!' I was on fire by now. 'I am not the club's bloody lackey-lad. You would not have told your last groundsman to do that, so don't tell me because I am not doing that job for you or any bugger else at this club!'

'You are,' he retorted. 'It's a priority job.'

'Then piss off and do it yourself or get Dyno-Rod in!' I concluded.

He was raging with temper himself by now and, as he was about to leave, he stopped and exploded: 'You will find yourself, one of these days, walking out of this club with your cards in your hands! You are not talking to me like that!'

'Well, sod off and do it now!' was my reply.

The next morning, he spoke to me as though nothing had happened and I concluded that when he had thought about it, he knew I was right, but that was when I decided I had had enough of the goings on at the Vale without the security of a contract and so I decided to force them to give me one.

When Doug came back from being sick, I told him about the incident with the chairman and said, 'When this business has blown over, me and you want a contract.' In due course, I approached the chairman and his reply was, 'What on earth do you want a contract for? You have got a good job for life here.'

'Well, Mr. Singer,' I replied, 'directors come and go and I want a bit more security than that given by word of mouth.'

'Well, Denis,' he said to me, 'no-one in the club will have a clue how to go about it. Yours is a very complex job indeed.'

'Then I will write one out for you,' I said.

'That sounds all right to me,' he replied, 'but I'm making no promises as to whether we shall accept it.'

I sat down at night and this was the contract that I wrote out:

'The hours of work will be 40 hours as it is for any other job and these hours shall be phased over 5 days but because most matches are played on a Saturday this will be deemed a normal working day, and time off during the week will be taken to compensate for working Saturday. For all the matches played during the week the hours worked shall be calculated at time and a half, and for Sunday and bank holiday work and any extra time worked during the closed season, this will be calculated at double time.

However, for all overtime worked no extra payment shall be paid but for such time worked time off in lieu will be allowed as already described. Time shall not be taken for any reason whatsoever on the day prior to a match, or the day of a match.

At the commencement of each season the groundsman will receive a pay increase in line with whatever the average increase is throughout industry.

In the event of termination of employment three months' notice will be required except in the case of any misconduct on the part of the groundsman in which case the club will decide.'

48

Well, that was the contract and I handed it to them on the day of a board meeting. Less than 10 minutes had elapsed before the chairman came into the tearoom where I was having a cuppa. He was beaming all over his face and said, 'Denis, you have done a great job with that contract and, as far as I'm concerned, I cannot see any problems, but I will talk to you in the morning after we have discussed it at today's board meeting.'

The next morning, just as he had promised, he came to see me.

'No problems with your contract, Denis,' he told me. 'The board are delighted with how you have set it out. Norman Jones will take it over to our solicitors this afternoon for them to look at and, if there are no problems, as soon as we get it back, the secretary and myself will sign it on behalf of the club and you and Doug will put your signatures to it, making it binding both ways. You and Doug will get a copy each and the club will keep its copy.'

It took less than a week to get the contract back from the solicitors and it was duly signed. I had never known them to act so quickly on any matter concerning me in all the time I had been at the club. Now, at this stage, readers may ask where on earth my brains were to draw up such a document, with all the implications concerning the overtime aspect. Well, the answer to that is quite simple. What I had written in the contract was the way I had been working and was what had been expected from me from the day I stepped into the club. I knew I was not going to get anything different however hard I tried, but I am not daft. That contract was a time bomb, ticking away in the directors' direction from the moment I signed it. Now I will explain this, as I did at the time to my assistant, Doug.

'Doug,' I said. 'This club will never again be able to abuse us the way they have done up to this time. Three months' notice suits us fine if ever we have to give our notices in. It gives us plenty of time to find another job. We did not get a pay increase last year and everyone else did, so now we will because our contracts say so. And, best of all, Doug, if they do not treat us properly, we will enforce our time off in lieu clause and that way they will have to fork out hundreds of pounds for all those jobs we do when we should be taking time off. And, I shall never shout or swear at any of those people up there and that way they will not be able to get us on the misconduct clause.'

Well, it did not take too long for that little time bomb to blow up in the chairman's face. Near the end of the following season, he came out to me one morning, really excited.

49

'Denis,' he said, 'I have some great news for you. The F.A. wants us to stage the Non-League F.A. Trophy semi-final here a week on Saturday.'

Well, a firm of painters had just moved into the Railway Stand to clean all the rust off the interior metalwork of the roof and then repaint it. The stand was in a terrible mess and I informed the chairman there and then what the foreman of the painting firm had already told me, that the painting of the stand would not be complete until dinner time of the Friday. This was the day before the big match. I also informed the chairman that we had a reserve match here on that same Saturday.

'Oh, don't you worry about that,' replied Mr. Singer. 'I will get Roy [Sproson] to play that somewhere else,' which would have been possible in those days because the reserve team was only operating in the Staffs County League. Mr. Singer left me in order to have a word with Roy, but he returned to say, 'Roy will have none of it and so we play here after the F.A. Trophy match, but to give you time to do a little work on the pitch and have a breather we will kick off at seven.'

'Mr. Singer, to get the stand clean,' I said, 'we shall have to work until dark on Friday night and then we will have to come about 6.30 on Saturday, which means we would have to do about fifteen hours on Saturday!'

'Well, Denis, for goodness' sake, don't let us down,' he replied. 'This is one of the biggest matches we have staged here and I want everything to be spot on.'

'Well,' I enquired, 'what shall we get in extra cash for all the hours and extra work we have got to do?'

'Nothing at all. You get your wages like everyone else in this club!' came the swift reply.

'But hang on a bit,' I said. 'This is an additional fixture and not a club fixture.'

'That makes no difference at all, Denis, and anyway, Saturday is a normal working day on your contract,' he retorted. After a lot of further discussion, he said, 'I will see you on Friday before we set off for our first team game.'

The Vale were travelling to Plymouth at about two o'clock and he was travelling with them. Well, he never came near me on that Friday and it was I who eventually went to see him.

He said, 'Denis, I gave you my answer yesterday and nothing has altered since then.'

More discussion followed, which got me nowhere, and his parting words to me were, 'Oh, I will see you on Monday.' Well, Monday came around and he duly came out to see me.

'You and Doug did us proud on Saturday, Denis,' he said. 'Everyone, and I mean everyone, was most impressed and very pleased with everything that was done. I bet you and Doug were tired to death on Saturday night.'

'You can say that again,' I replied. 'We were here from 6.30 in the morning until 9.30 on Saturday night and don't forget also we were here until 9.00 on Friday night.'

'Yes,' he said, 'I knew there was a lot of work to be done, but everything went off smashing,' and at that point he turned to leave.

'Hang on a bit,' I said. 'What about that extra money?'

'Oh, don't start that again,' he replied. 'I gave you my answer last week.'

More discussion followed, but this time it got a little heated and he asked me, 'How much do you think we should give you—£10 each? No chance,' he thundered, and once again he turned to leave me, but I stopped him in his tracks.

'Is that your final word, then, Mr. Singer?' I asked him.

'It most definitely is,' he said.

At that point, I reached into my inside pocket and pulled out my notebook.

'Mr. Singer,' I said, 'there is no match here now until next Saturday. At one o'clock today, Doug and I will be off and we will not be back again until Friday, the day before our next match!'

Now it was he who was fighting to control his temper.

'Don't talk so stupid,' he yelled at me. 'There may not be much to do on the pitch at this time of the season, but there's lots to do around the ground to prepare it for next season.'

'Then you can bloody well get someone else to do it,' I shouted.

I then shoved the notebook under his nose and, with great delight, I informed him of its contents.

'Ever since I signed the contract, Mr. Singer,' I said, 'I have kept a very strict record of all the hours Doug and I have worked and by calculating our overtime hours as per the contract, you owe me and Doug one hundred and eighty hours in lieu of such time worked!' And, now unable to contain my delight at the look on his face, I finished off with relish by saying, 'You were quite happy to quote the Saturday element of our contract last week. Now you can bugger off and think about all those hours you will still owe us when we come back next Friday!'

He left absolutely furious, but, a short while later, he came into the

51

tearoom where we were having a cuppa. He had a very angry look on his face and in a nasty tone of voice he said, 'Norman Jones will give you £10 apiece at dinner time, but you will have to sign a petty cash slip and pay tax on it.'

'Sod off,' I said. 'I see people go into that office every day of the week and come out with a fistful of money and never sign a slip. Ten quid each and no petty cash slip or no deal!'

That was exactly how this money was paid. Now £10 even in those days, was peanuts, but the purpose of the exercise was to win the battle of the contract and therefore ensure that the people running the club were now very aware we were no longer doormats.

11

Exit The Groundsman

From the day I had beaten the chairman over the contract issue, things were never quite the same between me and him and it all came to a head on a very cold and dreary, wet day at the end of November 1975. As I was about to take my lunch break that Wednesday, I was called into the secretary's office to see the chairman.

'There is a match out there, kickoff at seven tomorrow night,' he informed me, 'between the NatWest Bank and Barclays Bank. After the match, there is a buffet laid on in the social club at ten o'clock and you are quite welcome to come.'

I was dumbfounded, to say the least. We had just had six weeks of the wettest weather ever recorded up to that point in time and we had played nine games in that month of November. That was because we played a first team match one Saturday and a reserve team one the next, and we were also in the Northern Floodlit League, playing every other Wednesday night. However, by working our guts out, all had turned out well. We had not had one postponement, and there was the chairman telling me as late as that lunch time that there was a match to be played the following night. I was about to explode, but he cut me short.

'You know you don't own that pitch out there,' he said, 'and you are not going to dictate to us what goes on out there. I can see from the look on your face that you are far from happy about it, but this club has got to keep good relations with the bank in order to survive.'

Now, the daft thing here is that it cooled any anger which I felt. I went away thinking, no bank, no overdraft, no Vale.

It rained non-stop from midnight on the Wednesday through until four o'clock on the Thursday when the rain was replaced by one hell of a gale, but the pitch, much to my relief, had taken the water really well. The match duly kicked off at 7.30, with just three spectators watching! The final whistle sounded at 9.10 and Doug, his brother Terry, another helper and I spent time putting the worst of the divots back and then we commenced our rolling. The job had to be done immediately because of the risk of frost at that time of year and because we had a league fixture imminent.

The rolling of the pitch was the worst I had ever experienced in all the while I had worked there. We had to pull the roller down the pitch from the Hamil to the Bycars End while we were being blown about and struggling to keep on our feet. Coming back the other way, we had to fight our way through the gale and then, to make the job more difficult, it started to pour down with rain again. However, we completed the job and left the ground at about 11.45. I arrived home just before midnight. My wife opened the door to let me in and her first words to me were, 'Just look at the state you are in. I will finish up without a husband and the children without a dad!'

Now, I was very tired and completely worn out and wound up. In these kind of conditions, I tend to blow my top. However, on this occasion, I did not because, as I was about to, I caught the look on her face. It was the sort of look only those closest to you and those who think most about you ever give you. My wife and I are best mates and we always have been, and so I said nothing, but made my way into the bathroom to have a good wash, prior to a cup of tea and bed.

As I did so, I stopped to look in the mirror which hangs in our hallway. Well, as the old saying goes, every picture tells a story and, by God, that mirror told me one! I was as white as a bag of flour, haggard in features and wild around the eyes, just like a hunted animal. Instantly, I had known the meaning of that look which I had just seen on my wife's face and the mirror confirmed it. I went downstairs after my wash, got the pad and pen and wrote out my notice. I sealed it in an envelope, addressed it to the chairman and left it there ready to give to him in the morning. I have never felt so relieved as I did at the moment that I handed it in. I felt as though a great weight had been lifted from my shoulders.

The chairman came out to see me about eleven o'clock on the Friday morning and said, 'Well, everything went alright last night, Denis, and the pitch doesn't look too bad.'

I did not reply to that, but took out the envelope from my pocket and handed it to him and said, 'This is my final answer, Mr. Singer, to all the hassle that goes with this job. That is my notice.'

'Oh, well,' he retorted, 'we've been expecting something like this from you for some time, but you must be crazy to do it now the pitch is getting better all the time and you have almost cured the drainage problems. When we advertise this job in the "Sentinel", there will be a queue right down to Burslem Fire Station.'

At that point, he turned and left me. So there I was on my notice, but this was not mentioned again until about three weeks before I was due to leave. I was informed by a chap who was very close to one of the directors that only three blokes had applied for the job—one a building site worker, one a pottery worker and the one they eventually appointed, a landscape gardener. So much for Mr. Singer's queue! The chap who gave me the information also told me that the directors had already interviewed all of them in a café at Newcastle and were not very impressed with any of them, but he said, 'The directors are quite sure that you will not leave here and that you are bluffing in order to squeeze a better deal out of them.'

Only two days after he told me this, the first move started to try and get me to change my mind. 'No chance,' I told them, and so they appointed their new groundsman, Graham Mainwaring. When I met him, I thought he was a good man for the job and I worked with him at the request of the club for one week prior to my departing. Unfortunately, he did not last long at all. If they thought I was blunt and outspoken, they soon found out that he was more outspoken than me! Also, he was not a Port Vale man and he had gone there as the Head Groundsman with the understanding that he was going to have staff to work under him. In the event, he was replaced by my former assistant, Doug.

My length of notice allowed me to have a good look around the job market and I was not very impressed with what was on offer. You see, I wanted to try something completely different, but I did not realise at that point in time just how different my new job was going to be. Alderman Barber spoke to the Parks director, Mr. Jackson, on my behalf and all that was required was a phone call for me to be on my way for an interview with him. He did not beat around the bush. He told me that the job he wanted me to take on was the maintenance of the newly-constructed Hanley Forest Park, which had just been handed over by the contractors. He also told me that if my assistant, Doug, was looking for a job, he would also engage him to work alongside me.

'There is only one thing, Denis,' he said. 'We cannot match the wages which you are getting at Port Vale.'

At this point, I thought, my goodness, the park lads must be poorly paid. I hardly dared to ask for the amount, but, of course, I had to. So, I enquired, 'How much, Mr. Jackson?'

He replied, 'Well, because of your vast experience and because I really want you to sort this job out, I will put you on the top grade, which is £34.25.'

'Well,' I said, 'that's four pounds more than I'm getting now and I don't get paid any overtime.'

'Well, I have known you for a very long time,' he said, 'and I always thought you had a wise head on your shoulders, but I think you have been completely crazy to work the way you have done for that sort of money! And add to that the fact that you are one of the few people in Staffordshire who has the First Class Certificate in Turf Culture and Ground Management. Still,' he concluded, with a smile on his face, 'it makes it easier for me to offer you a job.'

'Well,' I said, 'I will accept your offer.'

As I was about to leave his office he said, 'If you do as good a job with the Forest Park as you have done at Port Vale, you will not be there forever,' and I was not. Eighteen months later, the area of the Parks Department that I had previously supervised became vacant. I applied and was appointed and so life turned a full circle, or almost, as you will shortly see.

The day of my departure from the Vale arrived and I went into the office to collect my final pay packets. There sat Mr. Singer.

'Well, I hope you are not going away from here blaming us for a rough deal,' he said. 'If you have had a rough deal it is as much your fault as the club's. You have put loyalty to the club and the job before yourself.'

I was absolutely stunned! I made my way to the sheds for the last time and sat down on the mowing machine with the thought going over and over in my mind, how on earth could they have someone putting complete loyalty to the club and the job and give him such a rough deal? The conclusion I came to was that people like that man do not give a toss about the Vale. They are only here on an ego trip. I locked the shed up for the last time and made my way in the direction of the main exit on the Lorne Street side. As I did so, I stopped and gazed at the empty terraces and I thought, next week that is where you will be, standing back amongst your own type, the people who really care about the Vale.

12

Almost Full Circle

I was just getting settled in my new job at the park, when one evening I picked up the "Sentinel". It was about eight days after I had left and there on the back page was the headline, 'Pitch Problems At Vale Park'. There was the manager, Roy Sproson, explaining how the new groundsman was working very hard on the pitch to combat the many problems. I was absolutely amazed! Roy and the coach, Reg Berks, knew how hard I had worked to put right the drainage problems because they knew what a mess those drains were in when I took over the job and they, above everyone else, knew the exact reasons for my leaving. And the pitch was not one of them. I have never walked away from any problems in my life and I did not walk away from one there. So, I decided to set the record straight by writing the following letter to the "Sentinel":

'I am surprised at some of the comments at Port Vale regarding the condition of the pitch and in particular the remarks of eight days ago that a lot of hard work had been done to iron out the snags. Surely Roy Sproson and Reg Berks do not expect perfect playing conditions at this stage of the season, after all the rain we have had this winter. Vale Park is still one of the best pitches in the country and I feel that the manager is trying to cry wolf for this slump in the team's performance.

When I left the Vale, out of sheer loyalty to the club I have supported all my life, I chose to say nothing about what led to my departure, but I can honestly say the pitch was not a reason. I cannot understand why the manager has waited until I have gone before making his remarks. My advice to him is to get on with the job of providing a team good enough to give some entertainment to the fans and do not go looking for scapegoats when something goes wrong by casting shadows on the good work of those who have done their best for the club. Best wishes to the team, the new groundsman and the best supporters in the world.'

In the days that followed the publication of my letter, I was amazed at how many people came into the Forest Park and met me on the ground at the Vale to shake my hand or pat me on the back for all that I had done there. I had total support from all these people who condemned the manager and his assistant for their comments. The conclusion I came to was that there had been a bit of a backlash somewhere and the manager had gone public with his remarks in order to cover things up on the club's behalf by suggesting that I had left because there was something wrong with the pitch—but he had failed miserably.

However, life is full of little twists and one day, after I had been left the Vale for about two years, I returned to my office at Burslem Cemetery to find on the desk a note asking me to ring Longton China.

'That's Arthur McPherson,' I remarked to someone nearby.

'He must want to ask me something about the Vale. Well, he can go and get stuffed. I want no involvement there!'

However, curiosity got the better of me and I picked up the phone and dialled. Someone then put me through to Arthur, who said, 'Now, Denis, don't bite my head off. Just hear me out. We are very concerned about the pitch and it's worrying Doug to death. He is a good worker but does not have your experience and I have a proposition to put to you if you will come and talk to us before Saturday's game.'

'Well, I'm not coming back as groundsman,' I retorted.

'Not even if we offer you a good wage?' he asked.

'No!' I replied.

'Then you must be doing very well where you are.'

'Not really,' I said, 'but I can go home at five o'clock at night a contented man, but anyway I will come and see you on Saturday afternoon.'

I went to see them on the Saturday and was invited into the boardroom. There I sat, at the big long table, looking straight into the eyes of that miserable sod, the ex-chairman, Mark Singer, who blurted out to me, 'We should never have let you go from here, we shouldn't.' But, before he could say anything else to me, Arthur McPherson cut him short by asking me, 'Do you want a whisky, Den?'

I replied, 'No, thank you,' and we got down to the business of talking.

'You know every inch of this pitch and no-one knows it better,' said Arthur. 'At a recent board meeting, it was suggested that we bring an expert in and if necessary put him on the payroll in order to sort out our problems, but I said I would have a word with you first. Of course, you will be paid for this and we are thinking in terms of £20 per week.'

'Don't talk so bloody daft,' I said. 'You can't afford that sort of money and I won't take it off you. Give me £5 for petrol and I will take you on.'

'Great!' they said and that was the end of that. As I turned to leave the boardroom, I glanced back at those smiling faces. You would have thought by their look that they had just signed the England captain on a free transfer. I thought, when I was here you could not treat me properly and you have spent the last ten minutes grovelling to me, you soft buggers, all of you. You could not run a piss up in a brewery.

So, life had gone virtually full circle. I was back in my old job at the Parks and now I had both feet back in at the Vale. The title that they bestowed on me was "Ground Adviser to Port Vale F.C.". I relinquished the title of my own free will in 1990 when I pointed out to the secretary that with two good groundsmen at the club, they did not require me poking my nose in. Now, people may ask here who the soft bugger was— me for refusing the £20 or them for offering it? My answer to that is quite simple. If I had accepted that ridiculous offer for doing such a small job, I would not have been any better than those who had given me such a poor deal when I was there and, in my book, two wrongs don't make a right and never will!

My dad relayed a story to me after he had been a guest of Mr. Singer during a game played at Southend, the town where my dad went to live during the last years of his life. He was just about to go into the football ground when Mr. Singer, who had spotted him, called out, 'Stephen, come in with us. It's my little treat to you for the days when you were our cheerleader and, more important, for all the wonderful work your son, Denis, did for us on the ground. Denis was a very hard man to understand and get on with. You never knew when you had got him, but, by God, we would never have let him go if we had known he was worth two men to us.'

Well, you never miss the water until the well runs dry, do you?

13

Rubbing Shoulders
With The Famous!

During my time at the club, I met three top entertainment personalities. The first one was Pat Phoenix, who was better known as "Elsie Tanner" of "Coronation Street". She visited the club when we played Stockport County in 1967, as she was the president of the County supporters' club. She was a great character who put herself about a lot during her visit, but there was absolutely no edge on her at all.

The next celebrity I met was Eric Morecambe of the famous "Morecambe and Wise Show". At that time, he was a director of Luton Town football club and came to the Vale when we played them. What a grand chap he was. The whole time before and after the match was sheer comedy! He was exactly the same funny man that you saw on television.

The last one I met was Elton John, the singer, and he visited the club when we played Watford because he was their chairman. Everyone in the club was talking about him for days before he came, but I am a Kathleen Ferrier and Mario Lanza fan and cannot stand the modern stuff. So, I had not a clue who the guy was. I was standing in the passage near to the chairman, Mr. Singer, when this fellow came charging through in the direction of the boardroom, with a silk scarf around his neck, a velvet bottle green suit, high heel shoes and a pair of big, dark glasses.

'Christ! Who the bloody hell is he?' I asked Mr. Singer.

'Hush, for goodness' sake, Den,' Mr. Singer said. 'You know damned well who he is! That's Elton John!'

'And who is he then?' was my next question, at which point Mr. Singer knew that I was not kidding.

'Denis,' he said, 'I thought I was a million light years behind the modern music scene, but you are on another planet altogether!'

14

Player Personalities

During my time at the Vale, I saw a lot of players come and go, but because it is my view that players get more than enough publicity, I am not going to write a lot about them in general, only those which, for one reason or another, stick in my mind.

One day, when I was working on the pitch, out came a tall, well-dressed and very smart-looking chap, wearing gold-rimmed glasses. He looked a million light years away from being a professional footballer. He came over to where I was working and we became engaged in football chatter. He was very keen to know all about the ground and why we were known as "Port Vale", since there was no seaport near us. There was no doubt about his place of birth. He was clearly Irish. After we completed our conversation, he left and, later in the afternoon, I went into the tearoom to have a cuppa.

'Have you met our new centre-forward, Den?' Lol Hamlett asked.

'No, I haven't,' I replied.

'Well, I saw him out there talking to you earlier,' Lol said.

'What? That toff with the Irish accent and gold-rimmed glasses, him a footballer? Never!' I replied.

'My friend,' Lol said. 'Never judge a book by its cover. That chap is Sammy Morgan and Gordon Lee has just signed him from Gorleston Town.'

Tommy McLaren was a super lad who loved Port Vale and he was a bugger for a joke and a bit of fun. He always appeared a tough character on the field, but, in fact, he was a very soft-natured and shy chap.

Ray Williams was another player who liked a bit of fun and was always taking the mickey out of someone, including me! Had Ray not chosen teaching for a career, I am sure that he would have played at a higher level.

Tony Lacey may not have been the most classy of players, but what a grand pro he was—a credit to the game, in every way. He gave his training one hundred percent and gave his all on the field. Also, he always tried to give sound advice to all the younger players.

Roy Chapman was another very dedicated pro, who never gave either his training or his playing less than one hundred percent. Some of the other pros. in the club said that he was selfish, but then there is a saying in football that all strikers are selfish.

Alan Boswell was, in my opinion, a player who had a rough deal from some sections of the supporters. He was, in fact, a most dedicated pro and on Friday mornings, before first team matches, he would come to me and ask, 'Den, can I do ten minutes or so in one corner with the ball and if I am making any sort of mess, I will move off.'

My answer to Alan was always the same, 'Yes, certainly you can,' because unlike some of the other pros. at the club, I knew that with him ten minutes meant just that. And if he was making a mess, he did not need me to move him off.

John Ritchie was a real character and a very tough one at that. I have never forgotten one night match in particular when John was playing full-back for us. I was sitting in the trainer's box with Len Graham and Lol Hamlett, and, every time John tackled, great lumps of turf were kicked out.

'I'll have to look at his boots at half-time,' Len remarked to Lol.

As we kicked off for the second half, Len turned to me and said, 'Ever likely he kicked lumps out of your turf in the first half, the daft sod's been out this afternoon and bought a pair of rugby boots! It's a damned good job the ref's not spotted them!'

When John left to join Preston North End, he gave those boots to me and said, 'Here, Den, you can have my boshookers!'

Bobby Gough was a smashing footballer and a very bubbly little character. Because of his skill, he should have played at a higher level, but I think his problem was the fact that he was a bit of a playboy outside football.

Mick Cullerton was another gifted player, who, to some degree, suffered the same problems as Bobby Gough. Had Mick got his head down and trained harder, it is my opinion that he would not only have played at the top level, but could also have played for his country, Scotland. However, it has to be said that he was struck down with a nasty illness, glandular fever, when he was with Derby County and the view the Vale had then was that if he did make a comeback, he would never be the same player.

Finally, I come to two players who went on to play at the highest level. Both of these lads I have mentioned elsewhere in my book, but I would like to add a little more about them.

The goalkeeper, Milija Aleksic, was a sullen lad in some ways, but was also honest, dedicated and hard-working. Because he was such an honest lad, he always spoke his mind and would not be pushed about. Because of this, he made some enemies in the wrong place and, I can say with certainty, that this cost him his chance to become a pro with the Vale, which was our bad luck and Luton Town and Tottenham Hotspur's good luck.

Ray Kennedy was a very shy lad in most ways, but he had a bit of a temper, which boiled over from time to time, and he also made enemies in the wrong place. In any case, no-one on the managerial side of the club rated Ray. I well remember, the first time that he was picked to play in the reserve team, he was so excited that he could hardly contain himself. That was quite unlike any of the other lads, on that day, who thought that they were fixtures in the team. I thought he had a most impressive game and that he would make a good centre-half, rather in the Jack Charlton mould. After the match, I was in the boot room, having a cuppa with those who ran the reserve team, and the chatter went a bit like this, 'Mel Lintern will make a great player, Malcolm Gibbon is going to be a good player, Alan Barker is going to make the grade, Gordon Logan is going to make a great player . . . '

At this point, I broke in and said, 'There is one player who has played out there this afternoon who I have not heard anyone mention.'

Bill Cope, our reserve team trainer in those days, was just about to sip his tea when someone asked, 'And who is that then?'

'Ray Kennedy,' I said.

Bill's tea went all over the floor.

'Stick to your ground work,' he said. 'Ray Kennedy is a bloody carthorse!'

Well, Ray's career is fixed in popular history now, but it just goes to show that even those who have played as pros. do not know everything.

I have a theory as to why these two lads went on to make the grade. They were down-to-earth lads who were prepared to graft away, they were not conceited and they neither smoked nor drank. Also, when most of the lads signed up for Sir Stanley Matthews, the greatest man ever to kick a ball, they thought that they were something special themselves and that success was sure to follow. Some of them as kids would have seen the pantomime "Aladdin and His Magic Lamp" and they probably saw Sir Stanley as their Aladdin.

15

Marvellous Managers!

The first two managers I worked under were Jackie Mudie and Sir Stanley Matthews and, without a doubt, they were the best of the lot. They were the only two who really made me feel that my job was important and that I was part of the club. Both of them were gentlemen, without question.

Gordon Lee was very straightforward in many ways, but he did not like me too much because I had and have always had pride in my work, most especially where Port Vale was concerned. But Gordon just did not give a bugger what sort of pitch the Vale played on—the type of football that Gordon encouraged did not require a decent surface!

I do not think that Roy Sproson and Reg Berks had a fair chance or a fair crack of the whip, but also I did not have a fair crack of the whip off these two gentlemen as you saw earlier.

It is fair to say that managers and groundsmen do not get on all that well. One of the main reasons is that the manager will always blame the pitch, whether it is the pitch's fault or not, after a bad game and groundsmen simply do not like that sort of thing. However, I will give two very good examples of why groundsmen don't see eye to eye with managers.

Imagine, firstly, if you will, the state of the pitch in the middle of February after the ravages of frost, snow and heavy rainfall. After a Saturday afternoon home match had been played at that time of year, I would go onto the pitch at 5 p.m. with my assistant and four helpers. I would leave at about 8 p.m. and return with the same helpers on the Sunday morning at about 8.30. I would work until 11 a.m. and then kick in early on Monday morning. At about 11 a.m., out would come the manager, who would say, 'Marvellous recovery it has made. You can't tell there's been a ball kicked on there on Saturday. It has recovered well. We're going to have a bit of a kickabout on there this morning.'

That kickabout would sometimes last longer than a league match itself and there I would be, left to put things right with just my assistant and no helpers.

My second example, which illustrates the gap between groundsmen and managers, concerns a match played on a Monday night versus Hartlepool, when we were running for promotion from the old Fourth Division in 1970. On the previous Saturday, we were due to play at home to Scunthorpe United in a league fixture, but this was postponed because of a blizzard. Nevertheless, out came the manager, Gordon Lee, and he looked at the terraces and said, 'Den, you'll get that snow off there, won't you, before Monday? I don't want us to have Monday's match called off for snow on the terraces.'

There came quite a bit more snow, leaving a two-inch covering on the pitch and quite a bit on the terraces, but I worked all day with my assistant, Doug, and quite a few volunteers to clear the terraces completely of snow. However, we left that which was on the pitch in order to protect it from the frost. At that depth of snow, I knew we would play because the ground was beautiful underneath. I had been given permission by the ground director to hire six chaps from the Parks Department to come in on the Monday and this I did at about 10.30 that morning.

Out came the manager, who said, 'For Christ's sake, don't shift any more snow from the lines! We're not playing tonight. We have got some injuries!'

'Gordon,' I said 'you'd better get a local referee to have a look and we shall carry on working on this pitch until he gives that verdict, because that is what I am paid for.'

'I've got Roy Capey coming in shortly,' he replied, 'but we're bloody well not playing!'

Roy came in and was amazed at the thought of any postponement, and try as Gordon did to twist his arm, he would have none of it.

Roy told them to get in the match referee, who was Mr. David Laing, and he only had to travel down from Preston. The directors and the secretary were desperate to play because there was a shortage of money in the club and the referee duly came, did his inspection and, without hesitation, declared the match to be on.

'Perfect conditions!' he said.

When he left, the manager was absolutely livid at me for the work I had done to get the match on. He yelled at me as he left, 'If we lose tonight, I'll blame you!'

We won 3-0, but the next morning, Gordon Lee came through the doors and brushed past me without a word. But if looks could kill I would have dropped dead there and then!

16

Dynamic Directors?

There are only three directors that I care to recall with any respect and two for other reasons.

Arthur McPherson was a Vale man from head to toe and he was a very down-to-earth chap. He treated everyone the same, including me. Whenever he spotted me, he would shout, 'Howdy, Den, how goes it out there?' All that Arthur ever wanted was success for the Vale and I felt very sad when the team trotted out at Wembley for the Autoglass Trophy final because he would have loved to have seen that.

Don Ratcliffe was another very decent and down-to-earth chap, who often came to the ground to do electrical work to save the club money. He was actually a qualified electrician as well as a garage proprietor.

Alderman Len Barber was my first ground director. At first, we did not get on very well. He was a very quiet, diplomatic type, whereas I was a little outspoken. I have always believed that if you think it, say it, and if it needs doing, get on with it and get it done. And I have never courted popularity. In my very early teens, my dad once said to me, when we were in the garden, 'You are a sullen, blunt, arrogant, little sod, you are,' and maybe that is how I came over to Alderman Barber.

The alderman never promised what he could not deliver, but it was all the little things that he did that are worth remembering. When there was snow and ice about during the winter months, he would very quietly come to me and tell me that he had arranged to have salt delivered. He kept good relations with the Parks Department, so that, if I needed to, I could borrow things on occasions. The morning after we had had a midweek game, he would say to me, 'I saw the lights go out last night. I was not being nosy, but I cannot rest until I've seen them go out, because I worry about you out there when you are working late.'

One of the things that I shall always remember best about him occurred on a Saturday afternoon before a match and after I had handed in my notice. I was going through the main doors just before the game and he quietly pulled me to one side.

He said, 'Denis, I am sorry things have not worked out for you here, I really am. Have you got a job to go to when you leave?'

'No,' I replied, 'but I will have by the time I have completed my three months' notice.'

He looked very concerned at that and further enquired, 'Would you like me to have a word with Mr. Jackson at the Parks Department?'

'It won't do any harm,' I replied.

As he left me, he once again said that he was really sorry and he meant it. That was on the Saturday afternoon and at about 10.00 on the following Tuesday I was called into the secretary's office to answer a telephone call from Mr. Jackson's secretary.

'Mr. Jackson,' she told me, 'would like to see you if you are interested in a job.'

Now, at that stage, I was not very keen. I wanted to try something different, but I did not realise just how different the job that he was going to offer me really was.

My next ground director, Len Cliff, was a nice enough fellow and in most ways was very straightforward. 'You and him will get on well,' I was told. 'He likes straightforward people and those who work hard.'

The first thing he said to me when he became the ground director was, 'I am going to make you the best paid groundsman in football when we have got the brass.' On another occasion he said, 'We're going to kit you up with some good equipment because the more time you save on the pitch, the more time you will have to do all the many jobs that need to be done, and time is money.'

However, the reality of the situation was quite different and whenever I mentioned spending money on anything, the answer was nearly always the same: 'Stony-broke we are, Denis. It's either shit or bust for us next season, matey!'

However, one thing that really stuck in my craw was when the board of directors resigned en bloc in 1970, leaving just Mr. Singer holding the fort. Mr. Cliff had been over from the Isle of Man (where he lived) for a few days and, on one visit to the club, he asked me if I would fill in the holes adjacent to the main gates because of possible damage to car exhaust systems. I was doing this job, when, late in the afternoon, he drove from the ground with his brother, Arthur (who was also a director), after a board meeting. As he passed where I was working, he completely ignored me! There was no excuse at all for this because I had to move my barrow to let him through. The next morning, I went into the ground. Lol met me with the words, 'Well, Den, we are in a right fizzing mess here now, aren't we?'

'Why?' I enquired.

'The whole board have resigned, leaving Mr. Singer on his own. Hasn't Mr. Cliff been to see you?'

'No, he has not,' I replied.

'Fizzing disgrace,' Lol said.

Compare that with the previous ground director and it is not hard to see who was the better man. You just cannot respect people like that, can you?

I first met Mr. Singer two days after I joined the Vale. He was introduced to me by the ground director, Alderman Barber. Mr. Singer came across as a fairly down-to-earth type of man, who expressed to me then the view that, because of my father's love for the club and my own lifelong support, I was the ideal choice for the job. It was when he became the chairman of the Vale, and I then saw a lot more of him, that I discovered the other side of the man. Had he have been as dedicated to the Vale as he said he was, he would surely have looked after me much better than he did. To put as much work into the club and do as many hours as I did, only to be the lowest paid member of the staff, was in my opinion a sick joke. He was a man who was never satisfied and did not care how many hours I worked, so long as what I did was costing nothing or very little. I think his motto towards me was, 'Today, you will do the impossible; tomorrow, you will perform miracles.'

The whinging which went on then about us being short of cash was very much as it is now and, in my view, that is why we only had gates of two and a half to four thousand. In any business, you have to speculate to accumulate and football is no exception. I can sum it all up best by repeating a conversation I heard between Mr. Singer and another director: 'All we need to do here,' he said, 'to keep our heads above water, is to sell a player every other year.'

I will leave the reader to decide whether I am being unreasonable or otherwise to Mr. Singer.

17

Unsung Heroes

I have explained earlier how my assistant, Doug Foster, came to the Vale, but I would also like to describe him as a person. He was a very hard-working chap, completely loyal to me in every way, and was one of the few people in the club that I trusted. When I rejoined the Parks Department, Doug initially went with me, but he could not settle there and he rejoined the Vale. When Graham Mainwaring, who succeeded me as the head groundsman, left, Doug took over, but he did not stay long at the Vale. I think this was because he found that when he had to deal with the people who were running the club, they were two-faced sods and he could not get down to doing the job the way that he wanted to. So he went down the road to our neighbours, Stoke City, to take over as the head groundsman from Len Parton, who had retired, and it was while Doug was there that he was offered and accepted a position as a sports hall warden. I still think he's a really grand chap.

I have mentioned Ann Povey earlier, but I would like to discuss her in more detail. She had once been described to me by the former groundsman as 'only the charlady'. What a load of rubbish! She was one of the hardest working people in the club. She washed, dried and ironed all of the club's kits and towels; she kept the main entrance hall and offices spotlessly clean; she laid out all the catering on match days and she set out everything in the boardroom before board meetings. She must have heard many of the club's little secrets, but never divulged any of them to other members of the back room staff. She was certainly a very dedicated and loyal member of the staff.

Lol Hamlett played for the club for short time, having come to the Vale from Bolton Wanderers in 1949. He moved to Congleton Town as the player-manager and rejoined the Vale in 1958, serving first of all in the capacity of trainer-coach and then as the physiotherapist. Like me, Lol was expected to perform miracles and he really did work very hard with few thanks. He was a good-living man and tried to set standards for the younger members of the staff. All in all, he was a great servant to the Vale.

I had met Norman Jones many times, long before I joined the club, and had always found him very helpful and friendly. When I collected my season ticket before the start of each new season, he always had time to discuss the coming campaign or any new signings that we had made. However, when I joined the club, I soon found out that Norman was not very well liked by some members of the staff and they were always stabbing him in the back. Now, I have met all the secretaries who have been there since Norman left and, with the exception of Andrew Waterhouse, Norman was by far the club's best secretary. Also, let no-one ever forget he gave Port Vale thirty years' loyal service.

The assistant secretary, who worked alongside Norman Jones, was a lady by the name of Maureen Jackson. She was a very pleasant and competent person who got on very well with all those working there. When Maureen left, Heather Green was appointed and she was very similar, but was much shyer. When Heather left to start a family, and right up to the time of my departure, no-one else was appointed, the work being shared between Norman Jones and Sir Stanley's private secretary, Wilf Coomer.

Bill Cope joined the Vale as a player from Bolton Wanderers in 1929. He was a local man and joined Bolton from Leek Alexandra. I never saw Bill play, but my dad, who did, said that he was one of the hardest tackling and toughest players that he ever saw. When Bill's playing days were over, he became the reserve team trainer and a very hard-working member of the back room staff. He was a really great servant to the Vale.

Reg Berks came to the Vale as a sweepstake agent. Then he became the social club steward, in turn the club's scout and then he moved on to the club's coaching staff. He was as straight as a ramrod and would never stab anyone in the back. However, because he never played football at a professional level, he was not accepted by some of the pros. who thought that he new nothing about the game. Well, I will give three illustrations of Reg's knowledge of the game.

The Vale were desperate to sign a goalscoring centre-forward to try and help them gain promotion from the Fourth Division and in came Reg one Monday, raving about this chap who he had seen playing for Southport—Jim Fryatt. 'Just what we want,' he said. 'Good in the air, can score goals with either foot and he has a nasty streak in him which all centre-forwards need.'

'No chance,' the club told him. 'They want £10,000 for him.'

Well, although he was then 26, he scored another 109 league goals before he retired.

Next there was Chris Nicholl, who was playing for Witton Albion, and

Reg was really keen to get him, but, because he wore contact lenses, they would not sign him. Well, we all know now that the same Chris Nicholl played for Northern Ireland and in the First Division for Aston Villa and Southampton.

Last of all, there was Jimmy Quinn who Reg wanted to sign. However, his request fell on deaf ears and we all know how Jimmy Quinn went on to play at a higher level and also for Northern Ireland.

Now don't tell me that Reg knew nothing about football!

It's funny how the club doctor rarely gets a mention and yet he is a part of the club, just as much as anyone else there. Our Doctor Glaister was one of the best and also one of the nicest men that I ever met in all my time at the club. Anyone could share a laugh and a joke with him, but none more so than me. One day, when he came into the club looking terrible, he said, 'I have been up all night with the trots and I have taken antibiotics which have stopped it, but I feel worn out.'

'Bloody hell, Doc,' I quipped, 'I am on your books, but if you cannot cure yourself, how will you cure me if I get that?'

Now, some doctors I have met would have not taken too kindly to that, but not so him. He burst out laughing and he departed with the words, 'Denis, you are a cheeky bugger, but you have made me feel better already!'

Keith Dale joined the Vale from our neighbours, Stoke City, in the capacity of pools promoter, and he did a great job before leaving to take up a similar job with Aston Villa.

Roy Cope succeeded Keith as the commercial manager in 1975 and also did a grand job. Before taking up this post, for a number of years Roy had been a very active member of the supporters' club and did most of the organising of the coaches for away trips.

Wilf Coomer came to the Vale as Sir Stanley Matthews' private secretary, but he soon became much more than that, helping out the secretary, Norman Jones, in a number of ways. He had earlier been a freight clerk with British Rail.

Jim Nixon was there when I joined the Vale, he was there when I left and he is still there now. Jim is one of the Vale's unpaid servants and you will find him these days in the ticket office, helping out when we have all-ticket matches. He is a very friendly chap and a real gentleman who has supported the club for some seventy years.

18

"Sentinel" Scribes

The first "Sentinel" reporter I met at the Vale was a chap by the name of Ken Whitmore. He was an arrogant little man, but those people in the club liked him because he always described things the way that they wanted them described. He was replaced by Bill Beckett, who was a grand sort, but again he wrote what the club wanted him to. Bill was succeeded by Chris Harper who was a different kettle of fish altogether. Chris only wrote about what he saw and, because of this, he was not the most popular reporter with those running the club. But, in my book, because of his complete honesty, he was the best reporter of the three. My mother used to urge us to tell the truth and would always say, 'The truth will stand when the world is on fire.' Therefore, I ask what good would it have been if Chris had reported otherwise because, after all is said and done, the spectators are watching the same match.

Ted Smith was the reserve team reporter when I was at the club and filled in sometimes when the first team reporter was ill or on his holidays. Ted also played cricket for Norton and by profession was a schoolteacher. He rose, I believe, to deputy head at one of our city schools. He was as straight as a gun barrel and if you said anything which he did not agree with, he would look you in the eye and tell you. So, my type of man, Ted was.

19

Regrets, I Have A Few

You might wonder whether I regretted going to the Vale as the groundsman. Well, firstly, if in 1966 I had signed for the Vale as a player of modest talent and had still been there in 1975, that would have been considered a fair stint. I would have loved to have been good enough to have played for the Vale, but I was not, so I did the next best thing and, on that count, I have no regrets whatsoever.

Now, to answer the question another way, if I judged my time there purely by the treatment I received from those running the club, my answer would most certainly be that I did regret going. But I do not look at it that way. I worked for the club, and here I stress the word "club", and not for those people who were running it. Over the years, too many people have entered the boardroom at the Vale to become directors and thought that they and they alone were Port Vale. The same can be said to some degree about some of the players and the managers who have been there. Well, this is not the case in reality. No man, be he the groundsman, the manager or a director is bigger than the club and the sooner some of the people at the Vale realise this, the better it will be for the club. Where would the Vale or any other club be without the people who pay their money at the turnstiles each match day? Or without the people who sell and buy lottery tickets? Or without those people who give many unpaid hours of work to the club?

I will now go on to give examples of where the Vale would be without these people. Many years ago, my dad told us about a mile of pennies in John Street in Hanley to help to get the club out of a desperate financial situation. He then told us about a silver sixpence collection for the same reason. Also, I can recall more recent times, like when we were expelled from the league in 1968 and had to apply for re-election at the end of the season. No director at the club wanted to sign the cheques for the wages or any other items and the supporters' club organised a concert in the Queen's Hall, Burslem, given by the Trafford Light Orchestra from Manchester. A lot of money was raised from this, and what about all the money raised for the purchase of Darren Beckford from Manchester City? Because the club said they had no money, we sold thousands of draw

73

tickets at £1 a book and the club were able to buy him and later sell him at a high profit. And what about the offer of cheap season tickets so that the supporters would buy them, thus enabling the club to pay the summer wages? But look at what happened in May 1996 when, because of a very good season financially, the club finally had the money to pay those wages and yet put up the admission price by 33%!

I say here and now that those prices were still below those of most other clubs and good value for the money, but try telling that to those people who have to pay for them. What will happen the next summer after we have a poor season? Would it not have been better for the directors to have put some money into the club during the summer and taken it out at a later stage, in order to have kept a realistic price for the season tickets? This would have avoided the huge increase which may yet have disastrous effects on the club at a later stage. Penny-wise and pound-foolish may yet prove to be the case! The club has just got to get closer to the supporters' club if it is going to survive the many changes which are at present taking place and I do not mean by this the planting of a stooge at the supporters' meetings in the form of an ex-director!

I make my own suggestion to the club. Why don't the entire board of directors meet with the entire committee of the supporters' club three times a year: before the start of the season, halfway through and at its end? This way, ideas could be discussed as to the raising of funds for the club and for better facilities on the ground, and all those little things that people moan about in letters to the "Sentinel" during the season could be ironed out. The club has got to build a bridge between itself and the supporters' club in readiness for the day when transfer fees will be abolished, as they surely will be. I think that if they could work along these lines, they will be in a much stronger position to meet all the many changes which are about to take place in our national game.

In making my suggestion for closer links between the supporters' club and the directors, I would like to point out that I have no vested interest in this suggestion because I am not and never will become a member of the supporters' club. I joined the Hanley branch of the supporters' club in 1950 and we used to have our meetings in the Glass Street Club in Hanley. I rarely missed a meeting. The committee members of that supporters' club were some of the most dedicated and nicest people who you could ever wish to meet: Bill Kirkham, the chairman; Clarence Kirkham, the vice-chairman; Albert Martin, the secretary; Ken Bootherstone, the treasurer, and Alderman Wood, who ran a newsagent's in Hanley.

To explain why I will never join the supporters' club again, I need to go back to events in 1954. When we went to the cup match at Cardiff that year, my dad did a lot of work in order to raise money for the supporters' club. My brother, Les, used to make Christmas wreaths for Dee's shop in Hanley and he had left over that year a large box of plastic flowers, which were white in colour.

'What are you going to do with those, Les?' my dad asked.

'Well, they will keep until next Christmas,' Les replied.

'I will buy them from you,' my dad said. 'I will get some black paint and put a few touches on them and then sell them as rosettes on the train down to Cardiff to raise a few quid for the supporters' club.'

That is exactly what he did. He hardly sat down on that outward journey as he walked along the corridors of the train selling the rosettes and he made £55 for the supporters' club, which was a hell of a lot of money in those days. In the next round of the cup, we were drawn at home to the holders, Blackpool. The tickets for this match were sold at a reserve team fixture and my brother, Eric, my dad and I queued from ten o'clock in the morning until 2.30 in the afternoon when the "sold out" notices went up and we had not got one ticket between us.

However, we decided to stay and watch the reserve match. We had not been on the ground long when up came two grubby-looking kids and said to my dad, 'Sell you two tickets, mate, for £5?' The admission price in those days was about three and sixpence (now seventeen and a half pence), but my dad did not hesitate to pay the £5.

On our way home, he said to us, 'There is only one problem now, lads. We need two more tickets if all four of us are to go. I have raised enough money for the Vale and so I think I might be able to get two if I approach the club.'

So, on the Monday after the Saturday sale, he went off to Vale Park only to be passed from one official to another and he finally finished up with the manager, Fred Steele. Fred verbally abused him something awful and because my dad hit back, he threatened to call the police and said, 'You are no different than any other supporter without a ticket, even though you may have raised a lot of money for this club, and, as regards your activities as the cheerleader, I think you must be bloody crackers going around wearing that bloody garb!'

When the draw with Blackpool was announced, the supporters' club was promised a generous allocation of tickets because we had about 400 members. Twenty-five tickets came through, with a promise of more if any were left! So, the committee of the supporters' club organised a draw to take place at the Glass Street Club over five nights. Now, because I was reckoned to be a lucky bugger in our house, I was nominated by my dad to go along and draw for all four supporters' club members in our household. I turned out to be a lucky bugger indeed because I drew out just one ticket!

Well, the Blackpool match came and went and a lot of our members left the supporters' club. At the end of that season, we had about £500 in our kitty and, after an open meeting, a proposal was put and carried that the supporters' club would purchase and distribute season tickets to pensioners. A letter was conveyed to the club informing them of our decision and a very prompt reply came back refusing our proposal. It told us in no uncertain terms that any monies which we had belonged to the club in whose name we had raised them. The letter also informed us as to how desperate the club was for money and finished by saying that Mr. Joe Machin, a director of the Vale, would come to Glass Street Club and explain to us just how serious their financial plight was.

Well, that was that for me and I never attended another meeting. I have written rather a lot on this topic and I have done so to illustrate just how far apart our club has been and still is from its supporters, and more importantly to bring home the point as to how vital it is to build that bridge between the two in readiness for when the transfer system is no longer a ready source of income for the club.

20

Presently Port Vale

Steve Speed is now the groundsman at the Vale and is well supported by his hard-working assistant, Shaun West. Assistants very rarely get a mention in any sphere of life, but are as important as any other member of the staff and Shaun is no exception. Steve took over from Bob Fairbanks, due to Bob's long spell of illness, and, like Bob, he is an excellent groundsman and a very hard-working chap. During the summer of 1994, Steve took the bravest decision that any groundsman could possibly take when he decided to have the whole of the pitch ripped up and reseeded. The previous closed season, the club had put in a complete new drainage system and Steve was not quite satisfied with the surface due to all the disturbance that had taken place. Well, I am sure that all who saw the pitch during the 1996-1997 season will agree that it has never played or looked better, and for that the groundsman takes the credit.

People may ask whether Bill Bell should be included amongst those who work at the Vale now. Well, I say that the chairman of any football club works just as hard as anyone else, sorting out all sorts of problems with the secretary and the manager, and so in that respect he is in there working. Bill has taken a lot of stick from some sections of the supporters, but, to those people, I say cast your minds back to the state that the ground was in when Bill became the chairman and look at it now. To me, it is a dream come true and so how on earth can supporters keep carping on about what has not been done? Remember the old saying, 'Rome was not built in a day.'

Mark Grew first joined the Vale as a goalkeeper from Ipswich Town and a very good keeper he was. When he left the Vale, he went to Cardiff City, but later rejoined us as the youth team coach. Up to now, he has done a pretty good job, but unless the club is prepared to let the lads in Mark's team progress into regular reserve team football and take a chance on some of them in the first team, then I think the man is wasting his time. Also, the club will not progress as the Liverpools and Manchester Uniteds of this world do.

Carol Brundrett has been at the Vale for over ten years and whenever the secretaries have departed, as they have done quite regularly over that period, Carol has taken on extra work until a replacement has been appointed. Carol's husband, Dave, also worked for the Vale, as the ticket office manager.

Rick Carter is the current physio and came to the club from Crewe Alexandra. He succeeded Jim Joyce who had moved on to Southampton. Physios work very hard in football clubs and they have to be very astute from time to time in order to be able to weed out the players who may be trying to con them over injuries. Before moving into football, Rick worked as a bank clerk and is a very hard-working chap with a good sense of humour.

John Rudge joined the club as the coach in 1980 and worked alongside the manager of that time, John McGrath. John Rudge joined the Vale from Torquay United where he had been a player and later the coach. He is the club's longest-serving manager and has done a great job.

Bill Dearden joined the Vale as the first team coach in 1994, having held a similar position at Mansfield Town. I remember seeing Bill play when he was at Sheffield United. He was the old-fashioned type of winger, who was fast and direct and had a good shot.

Jayne Pattison is a very dedicated Vale lady who has worked in the promotions department for about ten years. She worked very closely with Margaret Moran-Smith, but you never heard much mention of their valiant efforts. The same applies to Estelle Baggley and Michelle Dove who are long-serving members of the main office team.

Bill Lodey was the club's stadium manager before he became the secretary. He is also a lifelong supporter of the club and served on the committee of the supporters' club for many years. No better appointment has ever been made by the Vale because Bill can turn his hand to anything. During one closed season, when the club was building the disabled stand, I visited the ground on a Saturday morning and there was Bill, stripped down to just a pair of shorts, sitting on a huge digger, digging out the foundations for the building work. You name it and Bill will do it! However, in his new role, he really has his hands full, although I do not think the supporters realise just how important the secretary's job is at a football club or for that matter at any sporting organisation at any level.

Since I wrote the first draft of this book, there have been a number of departures, which sadly seems to be a way of life at the Vale. Tony Allan (the then secretary), Margaret Moran-Smith and Dave Brundrett have all resigned and Bill Lodey has moved from being the stadium manager into the secretary's post. The manager's seat in football is often referred to as 'the hot seat', but this cannot be true in the Vale's case. The hot seat must surely belong to the secretary. In fact, I would go as far as to say that this seat must be the hottest in the Football League because, in the last fifteen years, it has burnt the arse off twelve secretaries. I am sure that if the Vale made an application for inclusion in the "Guinness Book of Records", they would have no problems, for I do not think that any organisation, be it in sport or otherwise, could boast a better record! If I was the new secretary, I would pop into John Rudge's office for a chat, just to see how he has survived for fourteen years because I do not think that his seat can be much cooler. I think he must have his trousers lined with asbestos or he is kept so busy that he never sits down!

Although the above comments are made in a light-hearted way, deep down I feel very sad indeed at these departures and about other things which are happening in the club, for it is these things which the public are talking about rather than the team. And this is why our gates are down to such a large extent. This is surely proof enough to those people running the club that it belongs as much to the supporters as it does to them. To those people running the club, I say this, try running the club on the present gates and see just how far you will get.

An even worse situation developed after we had performed awfully and lost 2-0 at home to Crystal Palace on Tuesday 16 October 1996. There was a demonstration outside the main entrance. 'Sack the board! Sack the board! Bell out! Bell out!' was the chant from some of the disgruntled fans. Two days later, Mr. Bell announced that he was quitting and that the club was up for sale. He said that the sale had to be completed within seven days or he would close the club down. So there they were once again, the terrace undertakers, ready to read the last rites and bury the corpse, but as has happened so many times in the club's history things did not turn out quite like that. On the following Saturday, Mr. Bell withdrew his threat, thus allowing more time for a possible buy out, and that same day, the team produced a great result by winning 1-0 at Wolverhampton Wanderers.

That's the way to answer the people whom I have labelled 'the terrace undertakers'. That label is given to those media men who were asking on the local radio, 'Has anyone out there got five bob to spare? If so, you have to pop along to Port Vale and buy them out!'

That same label is also applied to the people who go round spreading stupid lies about things which are supposed to be going on behind the scenes. Some of them said, 'It's finished, this club is. It won't last the season!'

Finally, I will pin the same label on to those supporters who go around telling everyone what a good manager and chairman the club has when the team is doing well. They sing their heads off at matches: 'We have got the best team in the land!' Yet they boo the same people when things are not going well. Yes, I know it's expensive to follow your team and very frustrating when things are not going well, but it is no less frustrating for the people who are running the club, especially in today's tight financial climate. So, as far as I am concerned, so long as there is no corpse to bury, in the form of our club, I don't give a bugger. Long live Port Vale, I say...

21

Family Fortune

Everyone knows that my dad was the cheerleader and so nothing more needs to said about him. My late brother, Eric, was the biggest Vale fan of the lot in our house and travelled hundreds of miles to watch the Vale play. It was at the Vale that Eric passed away, in the vice-presidents' lounge after watching the team play and beat Barnsley 2-1 on a Monday night. I had just returned home from watching the match that night when the phone rang and I answered it. It was my youngest brother, Len, who informed me that Eric had passed away. What a sad moment that was, but even sadder still for our Len because he had travelled miles with Eric from a very early age to watch the Vale play. On the night that Eric died, Len was waiting in his car on the club's car park to take him home after Eric had had a cup of tea in the vice-presidents' lounge. What a shock it must have been when a club official went to the car to inform him what had happened and, even more to the point, what an awful and sad journey he must have had on his way home. However, I console myself with what Eric said only a few weeks earlier while we were at the Vale watching a reserve match on a cold December night. He looked really ill and I said to him, 'Don't you think you would be better by a warm fire than standing here frozen to death?'

'Den,' he replied, 'I know what the score is with me health-wise, but I could just as easily die sitting by the fire and I will tell you this—if I die here, watching a match that is, rest assured I will have died a happy man.' And with the wave of his hand in the direction of the Bycars End, he concluded, 'Just have some of my ashes scattered there and some at Norton Cricket Club,' which was another of his favourite haunts.

That is exactly what Eric's wife, Joan, and I did. And I tell you there have been some bloody great goals scored at that end since those ashes went on! I am not kidding!

My wife, Mable, is not interested in football and cannot understand what all the fuss is about. She does not know why grown men come home with long faces when the team has lost and she has had a lot to put up with all these years listening to me ranting and raving on about football and coming home with a long face when they have lost.

Neither of my daughters is interested in football, although I thought I had got my elder daughter, Carol, hooked during the Autoglass Trophy run, but her interest faded away and has not returned. I did manage to get my younger daughter, Jackie, to one match by filling her pockets with sweets and crisps, but, once her pockets were empty, all I could hear was, 'I am bored, Dad. I am cold, Dad,' and that was that for her.

Although I am the ex-groundsman and my father was the cheerleader, my only son, Robert, answers, if I ask him to go with me to the Vale, 'Me, I'm not soft like you. I would rather stop at home and watch paint dry.' That is even though Robert worked at the Vale for two years! Never mind because he has two little lads, Lee and Sam, and it will not be long before I rope them in!

At present, I do have one success story and that concerns my other two grandsons, David and Anthony. I have succeeded with both of them. They are both members of the Junior Valiants Club and season ticket holders, and this is no mean achievement because my son-in-law, Paul, who is their dad, and indeed all of Paul's family are Stoke City supporters! Here, I hasten to add, there is nothing wrong with them being Stoke supporters. I really do hate that small minority of people who go to the Vale and at every home match set up the chant, 'We hate Stoke.'

Of the others left in my family, my sister, Jean, is a keen Vale supporter and my brother, Les, is also very keen. And then there is me. I am and I have been a season ticket holder for a number of years. However, I have switched from the Family Stand to the Railway Stand into almost the same position that I occupied when I purchased my first season ticket in 1951. As I said earlier, till death do us part and I will always feel that way.

If our club ever reaches the top division and starts to win things, I hope I shall live forever. An ugly sod I'll be by then, but some people think that now! But I don't care so long as I have two eyes to see the Vale play and a voice to cheer them on with. The legs will not matter because some member of my family will push me to and from the ground. If they don't, I'll cut them out of my will and I'll leave my money to the club! That way I know that I shall get to and from the ground because those buggers at the Vale will do anything to get a few bob into the coffers!

22

The Top Team

At the end of every season, supporters are asked to vote for the player of the year. Well, I am now going to attempt to do something different. I am going to name my best Vale player over the last fifty years and my best Vale team over the same period. This is purely my personal choice and I have no doubt that other people will disagree with it. There is a lot of sentiment in football and the older we get, the more sentimental we become. Some of the names which appear will be purely for sentimental reasons, but I shall go into the merits of each selection. The team I have chosen is:

1
K. Hancock

2   3
S. Turner   N. Aspin (Captain)

4   5   6
H. Poole   R. Sproson   T. Miles

7   8   9   10   11
C. Askey   M. Foyle C. Pinchbeck K. Griffiths D. Cunliffe

Ken Hancock always seemed to enjoy his game and almost all of the time he seemed to play with a big smile on his face. He was a smashing keeper!

Stan Turner was a good two-footed player, who was as hard as nails and as cool as a cucumber under pressure. He followed the motto 'They shall not pass' and very few did!

Neil Aspin is a credit to the professional game and he never stops working. If the Vale were losing 5-0, Neil would still be going full steam.

Harry Poole is my choice as the best Vale player over the last fifty years. Harry could have played at the top level. He had good balance and two good feet and was a lovely passer of the ball. Above everything else, Harry had a great temperament and you never saw him in trouble with the refs for bad mouthing or kicking players up in the air.

Some people in the club went on about Roy Sproson having one foot, but I never remember him having any trouble with this when he tackled opponents. Roy was rock solid in the air and you never saw him give the refs any trouble or go about kicking opposing players up in the air. He was a great servant to the Vale and could and should have broken Jim Dickinson's record for one club appearances. However, due to the extreme jealousy in the club, Roy was robbed of this. I know because I heard many of the nasty things that were said regarding this and said by players of far less ability than Roy. Therefore, both the club and the man were robbed of a richly deserved honour.

Sentiment played a large part in my choice of Terry Miles alright. Not even Terry himself would have claimed to have been the best wing-half, as they called them in those days, but what a dedicated and loyal lad he was to the Vale. He would run himself into the ground for them and, if Terry was a player now, no manager at the Vale would have to worry about him pedalling his wares under freedom of contract. When he left the Vale, he was upset but not bitter. I met him outside on the day that he was given a free transfer and he said to me, 'Den, Port Vale is and will always be to me what Manchester United is to Manchester people.'

Colin Askey was a good two-footed player and an excellent crosser of the ball. Once he got past the full-back, he took some catching!

Martin Foyle is another Vale player who could and should have played at a higher level. Martin is a super player and one of John Rudge's best signings.

There was loads of sentiment in my choice of Cliff Pinchbeck, due to those two wonderful games that I saw him play, one against us and one for us.

Ken Griffiths was a lovely ball player and a great passer of the ball. He could and should have played at a higher level.

There was plenty of sentiment involved in the choice of my final player, "Dickie" Cunliffe, as we all called him. He was all heart and guts and would run all day. My best memory of him is in a cup tie played at West Ham in 1955. We were 2-0 down, but Dickie played a blinder for us and earned us a replay, which we won 3-1.

The players that I have named as my team over the last fifty years are by no means the only players whom I remember with great affection. There have been many players, both past and present, who have given me many hours of great entertainment, but to name them all would require a whole book. The players in the team that I have named are the ones, for one reason or another, that I shall always remember best and were chosen for this reason. The younger supporters of today will not remember most of the players that I have chosen and I am sure that a lot of the older supporters will disagree with some of my selections, if not all, but we all see things in our own way.

Now, who would I like to manage my team? Without question, it is John Rudge. Yes, I know John Rudge has his critics and when we lose two or three games on the trot, I criticize him just like the rest, but just look at the man's record since he became our manager! We have seen more good football played and have had more success and fun during his time as the manager than in the whole of my previous years as a supporter. I just hope John remains with us for a long time to come.

Throughout my book I have mentioned many names and have done so with great deliberation because football is a team game. Well life is, is it not? In life, people need people and football clubs also need people, especially those who are often referred to as 'stalwarts'. Almost every name that I have mentioned is or has been a stalwart. To those still there whom I have not mentioned and to those who have been there and have now gone, I say that you are and have been part of that big team and that you are no less important if your name does not appear here.

I would like to complete my book with my two most outstanding memories. The first one was that wonderful afternoon when Cliff Pinchbeck scored a hat trick on his debut. The second was of the feeling at 4.45 on 3 June 1989 when the ref put his whistle to his mouth, raised his arm in the air and blew for full-time, which signalled Vale's promotion to the old Second Division by beating Bristol Rovers 1-0 in the Play-Off final. I was standing alone in Lorne Street Paddock and I was glad of that because I was so full of emotion that we had made the big time again that I think had anyone spoken to me at that time, they might just have seen a grown man cry. And I was not the only one feeling that way!

When a new ship is launched, the words are said, 'May God bless all who sail in her.' I say may God bless all those who support the Vale and those who once supported them but have now passed on.